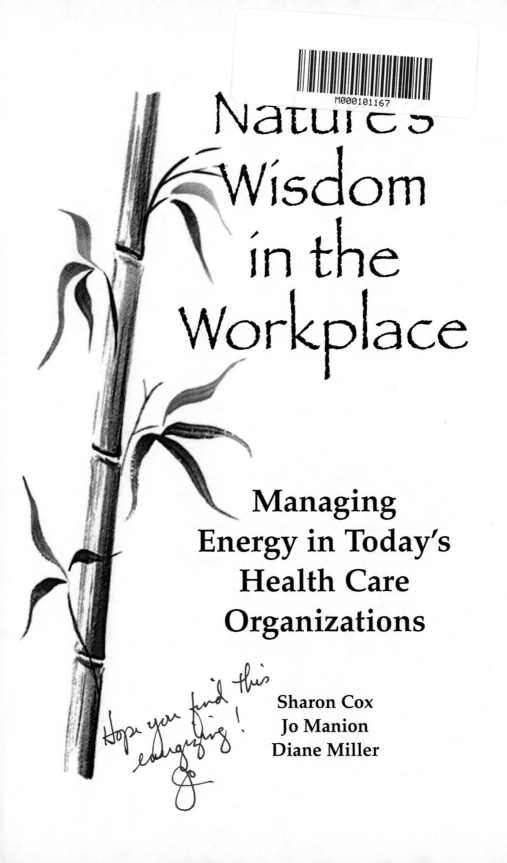

Nature's Wisdom in the Workplace

Managing Energy in Today's Health Care Organizations

Sharon Cox
Jo Manion
Diane Miller

Hope you find this energizing !

Jo

Cover design by Karen Saunders.
Cover illustration by Joyce M. Turley

Printed in the United States of America.

Library of Congress Control Number: 2005920770

ISBN 0-9764435-03

To contact the publisher: SynergyPrs@aol.com

Synergy Press
10277 Scarborough Road
Bloomington, MN 55437

Contents

Acknowledgments

We are grateful to Nancy Post for her willingness to share her knowledge of the Five Element Model with us. Her seminars and coaching have influenced our work as consultants over the years. A special word of thanks is also due to our dear friends, Lois Hybben-Stehr and Jennifer Jenkins, for their contributions to this manuscript. Lois shared her lessons learned on how to close a hospital and Jennifer, with her wonderful Metal energy, shared her thoughts in Chapters 8 and 11. Our friends, Lynn Anderson Rekvig and Dawn Sorenson, added their ideas to the Fire energy chapter and managed to have a party in the process, given their affinity for that energy.

We thank our professional colleagues in the United States, Canada, and England, who have participated in workshops over the last several years and illuminated our understanding of this model. Their enthusiasm for the richness and usefulness of this model, both in the health-care workplace and for personal balance, has been a source of inspiration. Their requests for more information and their eagerness to see us publish have been very encouraging.

We want to specifically thank the nurse managers and department directors at Sarasota Memorial Hospital, Sparrow Health System, St. Alphonsus Medical Center, and Genesys Regional Medical Center who have played a key role in providing many of the examples used to illustrate the use of this model in organizations. Norma Hagenow, Elizabeth Henry,

Carolyn Corbett, Mary Nolan, and Cindy Schamp have embraced the concepts in the Five Element model and supported their department managers in learning the model and, in so doing, have broadened the scope of our teaching.

Our acknowledgments would be incomplete if we did not mention the enthusiastic support of our friends on this journey...Gwen Sherwood, Sherry Bartels, Kay Hunt, Barbara Noble, Amy Brennan, Pat Potter, LeAnne Dougherty, Joe Krzyzanowski, and Linda Conner, who asked about our progress with this book and read our first rough drafts. Beth Burgan, Cathy Whitaker, Vicki Lachman, Tim Porter-O' Grady, Lynn Whisman, and Rosemary Peterson have been cheerleaders for this project over the years. Their periodic words of encouragement have been fuel for the fire to sustain this effort.

A special word of thanks is due to our editor, Barbara Munson, for her investment in this labor of love, her insights, and her suggestions along the way. It has been a pleasure to work with such a dedicated professional. We appreciate her genuine desire to make the topic of Chinese medicine understandable to the general public.

—The authors

I am grateful to my parents who taught me to follow my dreams and who were there for me as I first undertook the learning of the Five Element Model. I am grateful to my two grown children, Rob and Christine, who encouraged my writing even though they were not so sure what I was writing about at times. A special thanks to Val for helping me "go with the flow" and find that writing could be easier and more fun than I thought. The moral and logistical support provided by my husband, Jim, has been priceless. We have worked our way through all five of the energies at various times in this process and without his help this project would have never reached completion.

—**Sharon Cox**

As always, I thank my husband, Craig, for his steadfast support and patience with my work! His constant source of love and encouragement when I am immersed in this kind of project makes it possible for me to write. Additionally I want to offer a heartfelt "thank you" to my two coauthors, Sharon and Diane. Not only have they made this a wonderful journey, they have both been instrumental in increasing my understanding of this model over the years.

—**Jo Manion**

Thank you to Crystal, Peter, Gale, Joe, Carol, Carl, and the AZ Cowpokes for holding the hope that our dreams for this book would come true. Their support never wavered through the ebb and flow in our process. Thank you to Jake, Beth, Grace, and Val, who helped me understand more about the essence of my life journey and find the true teacher inside myself.

—**Diane Miller**

Preface

The relevance of ancient wisdom to the demands of life in the twenty-first century sparked our initial interest in how Chinese medicine might serve as a framework for understanding the complexities of organizational life. With technological, scientific, and medical advances coming at warp speed, we were impressed to see technology increasingly blending with ancient wisdom to achieve wellness.

At a neighborhood clinic in Seattle, alongside the latest in ultrasound equipment, an acupuncturist inserts needles in a patient to relieve a migraine headache. A cancer patient at a hospital in New York undergoes chemotherapy with highly sophisticated drugs, and also uses massage and the martial art of t'ai chi to augment the healing process. Indeed, some six hundred million people in the United States annually visit non-conventional healers and spend more today on "alternative" medicine than on western allopathic approaches to their health care.[1]

Does this overwhelming interest in non-invasive, wellness-focused interventions illuminate our perceived inadequacy of contemporary medicine's approach to health care? Or, can it be that Chinese medicine makes sense in modern times? That there is an innate need for, and connection with, the sense and symmetry of the fundamental principles of energy and healing evident in nature and formulated centuries ago? We decided to find out.

As organizational development consultants, we were intrigued with the implications of Chinese medicine in our own work with organizations involved in mergers, downsizing or striving to "do more with less." Through the work of Nancy Post, an organizational development consultant in Philadelphia who is also an acupuncturist, and her colleagues, we learned that Chinese medicine offers a practical and comprehensive framework for dealing with the demands of organizational life.

We were particularly drawn to this idea because of our backgrounds in health care and our awareness that, like the human body, organizations suffer disease and produce symptoms. As consultants and advisors to organizations, our first entry into a system is often to deal with uncomfortable symptoms that the organization can no longer tolerate. To our frustration, the medical model of identifying symptoms, making a diagnosis, and eliminating symptoms has been insufficient in dealing with the myriad issues involved with organizations undergoing major change internally and whose external forces are in constant flux. More than once we asked ourselves, "How can we get a handle on what's really happening here? How can we find a way to help?" It was with these questions in mind that we entered into a year-long training experience offered by Post and got our introduction to the ancient wisdom of Chinese medicine.

From that experience, we discovered a new model that offered a practical framework for proactively dealing with the issues our client organizations were facing—ranging from individual to system-wide issues. In our day-to-day work, emotionally committed to our clients, we often reached the point of exhaustion and discouragement. We found that our concerns were shared by many leaders in organizations today. These concerns are as varied as: Why do I feel exhausted at the end of the day although I don't feel like I accomplished anything? How do I balance and maintain my energy so I can continue to be effective in this setting? How do I replenish myself when I feel like I have nothing left to give? What can I do to take better care of myself when my daily work life feels so out-of-control? How do I intervene with myself to build my endurance levels during stressful times?

Everyone who works with groups or teams of people has struggled with these concerns on occasion. In some groups the problems seem constant! We must ask: What's the best way to get the group started? How can I move the group beyond the complaining and wallowing in their misery to taking action and accomplishing their work? Why is there intense "in-fighting"? How can I get the group focused and directed on its important work? At the organizational level, the concerns are very similar. How can we get employees fully engaged in the workplace and committed to the direction of the organization? Why are absenteeism rates so high? Why are so many executives, managers, and employees out sick with stress-related illnesses? How can we stay focused on one or two priorities when so much needs to be done now? What can we do to provide support for employees and managers without falling into the trap of entitlement? What are the most helpful ways of supporting people through the major changes that create new and difficult realities in their workplace?

The new model we learned about, the Five Element model of Chinese medicine, sheds light on all these issues and more. Throughout the training phase of our learning, we were continually amazed with the richness of the model, adding layer upon layer of understanding about energy, balance, and imbalance. We discovered that our own energy and enthusiasm in our work returned, a result of excitement in finding new ways to help our clients. Our subsequent use of this training and the insights gained provided the impetus for this book.

Our intent here is to share what we have learned and offer this approach to others interested in enhancing their effectiveness as leaders, managers or change agents in organizations. While it is not our intent to offer an in-depth understanding of traditional Chinese medicine, we do hope to convey the fascinating elegance of this model and the powerful learning that this ancient wisdom offers. Those who grasp the beauty of this model will hopefully pursue an ongoing practice in applying these principles, on both a professional—and a personal—level. Far from being a quick fix or temporary technique, like so many fads popularized in western culture, this model is more than five thousand years old. Its relevance to today's issues is nothing short of extraordinary.

* * *

This journey into Nature's Wisdom as reflected in traditional Chinese medicine is divided into three sections. First is a description of the Five Element model, which includes Five Energies and Twelve Key Functions as recognized by the Chinese in formulating their belief system for health and well-being. Here we review principles and terminology that make up the framework of the model and highlight these discussions with a few charts and diagrams for those who are visual learners.

The second section offers a more in-depth look at each of the five energies the Chinese see as essential: Water, Wood, Fire, Earth, and Metal. We look first at how they are manifested in the mind/body/spirit of individuals and then at how these energies are manifested in groups and organizations.

The final part of this journey is a consideration of several common work/life issues and the various applications of this model for leaders, managers or consultants interested in increasing effectiveness or organizational development. A chapter on increasing our personal capacity through self-care is offered. Tips for troubleshooting common group problems, based on over ten years of experience each of us has had with this model, also are covered.

The Five Element model engenders a sense of wonder in its completeness and symmetry. We invite you to enter into the study of this model with us and prepare to shift your view of the world, the way you see your role in organizations, and perhaps even the way you manage your own energy! Just as holistic approaches to health care complement the advances in medicine, so might the principles of Chinese medicine enable us to have healthier organizations—however downsized, flattened, integrated or re-designed they might be.

—**Sharon Cox, Jo Manion, Diane Miller**

1

What Is the Five Element Model?

Sharon Cox and Jo Manion

Organizational life today is full of unprecedented challenges. Internal and external change is occurring at breakneck speed, taxing even the most resilient of leaders and employees. Uncontrollable and unpredictable external market forces and changing governmental regulations create a sense of instability in even the most isolated and secure of organizations.

Fundamental changes are sweeping through the internal environment as well. No longer are we simply "tweaking" the system by creating new positions, adding variations of previous services or revising our documentation forms. Instead, health care organizations are changing fundamentally. Every aspect—from the internal culture and how people work together to where the work is actually being done—is being affected by change. Entirely new approaches to work are being sought and even the basic organizational structural unit, the *bureaucracy* itself, is being questioned as to its effectiveness in today's world.

The results of this chaos vary from community to community. Some organizations are actually thriving, at least it appears so on the surface. They are gaining market share and increasing profits. New services are being added and additional facilities acquired, and fuller integration across the continuum of care is being achieved. But the cost to their people and customers is often significant. For many organizations, absenteeism has never been higher or employee morale lower. Facilities are experiencing a true dichotomy—rapid and costly turnover of employees and managers on the one hand, and increasing entitlement and lowered productivity of remaining employees on the other.

There is less engagement and support from people in the organization at a time when full and complete commitment from employees is the only resource powerful enough to master the changes required. Some organizations have faced these changes and emerged healthier, with employees who are more resilient and adaptable, more able to cope with change.

Inside many organizations today, however, the challenges have exacted a heavy toll. In fact, the situation may be like the unfortunate patient who, having undergone the recommended surgery and treatment, dies anyway. The surgery itself was a success, but the patient was so debilitated that he or she could not survive the radical procedure prescribed.

Energy—

The Chinese recognized five primary forces in nature—water, wood, fire, earth, and metal, which helped explain the world around them. They call the five energies "elements." The term "element" in the Chinese belief system does not refer to a "substance," as we might think of it, but rather to a life force or power observable in the universe and in an individual.

What does this have to do with Chinese medicine? For most of us, the phrase itself brings to mind images of acupuncture needles or Chinese herbs. How these images could possibly relate to organizational life is quite a stretch. Yet, within Chinese medicine lies a beauty and symmetry of understanding that provides a valuable framework for dealing with the multiple challenges of today's world. Understanding a few fundamental principles will shed some light on these seemingly disconnected ideas.

* * *

Around the time of the ancient Egyptians, during the third or fourth millennium BC, the Chinese formulated a system for understanding the world around them, including the changing of the seasons, the light of the moon, and the cycles of night and day. This system also provided ways to maintain health and wellness in harmony with nature.[1] The Chinese recognized five primary forces in nature—water, wood, fire, earth, and metal, which they called the Five Elements. The term "element" in the Chinese belief system does not refer to a "substance," as we might think of it, but rather to an energy or power observable in the universe.[2] The Chinese believe that the universe was formed by a massive ball of Fire, which cooled and created the Earth. Eventually Earth's core solidified into minerals and precious metals deep under the surface. These metallic ores and minerals underlie river channels and give Water its direction and nourishing qualities. Water seeps into woods and fields, allowing plant life to grow. As the Wood is burned, Fire is created, which then becomes ash to nourish the Earth, and the cycle continues.[3] The Chinese referred to this cycle as the Creation cycle, or Shen cycle (refer to Figure 1-1).

Figure 1–1: Creation/Shen Cycle

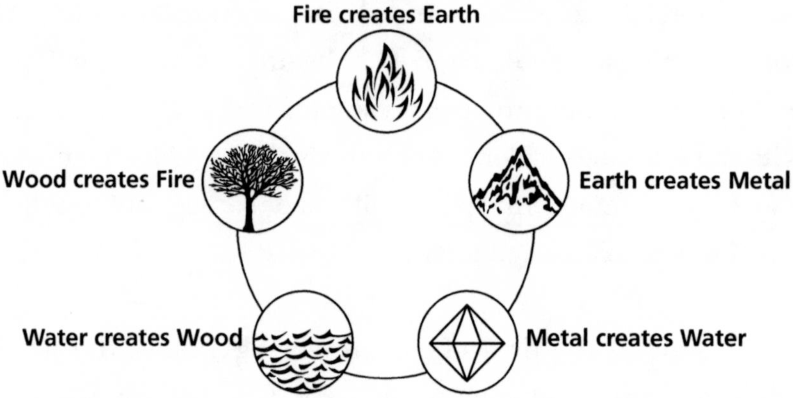

Fire creates Earth

Wood creates Fire

Earth creates Metal

Water creates Wood

Metal creates Water

Each element generates the next element and is sustained by the one preceding it. For this reason the Chinese sometimes refer to one element as being the "parent" of the other, in that each element feeds and nourishes the next element. In this way, Water is the parent of Wood, and Wood is the parent of Fire, and so on through the cycle.[4] Understanding this will become more important as we move into application of

Creation Cycle—

explains a way the five energies relate to each other. In this cycle, each energy is fed by the preceding energy or consumes the energy of the parent element so that it can exist.

the Five Element model, but for now just recognize that there is a natural progression of the energies and that the cycle continually repeats itself. This is often referred to in Chinese writings as "the unending cycle." Note that all of these Five Elements are essential to the support of life itself and no one element is more important than another. They are inseparable and constant, and life as we know it could not exist without each of these elements.

As they harvested their crops the Chinese could see this Cycle of Creation taking place—birth, growth, ripening, harvest and decay—each phase generating the next phase (see Figure 1-2). They noted continual movement, but it was not brought about by force. Everything comes of itself at the appointed time.[5]

In observing nature, the Chinese also recognized how the Five Elements could serve to balance or control each other. Water, when poured over Fire, quenches it. Fire can be used to melt Metal, and, if Metal is formed a certain way, like an ax, it can cut Wood. Wood, in the form of trees, plants or crops, pierces the Earth, and covers the hillside, keeping Earth from eroding. Earth when shaped as a bank or sandbag, can absorb and redirect Water.[6] The Chinese referred to this as the Control cycle or K'o cycle (see Figure 1-3). These two cycles, the Creation (Shen) cycle and the Control (K'o) cycle, work in concert with each other to maintain balance in the universe and in the human body as well. Chinese medicine is based on the belief that these same primary energies are at work within human beings and the same principles apply. Thus, "health" in an individual results from a dynamic balance of each of these five energies.

Figure 1–2: Creation Cycle

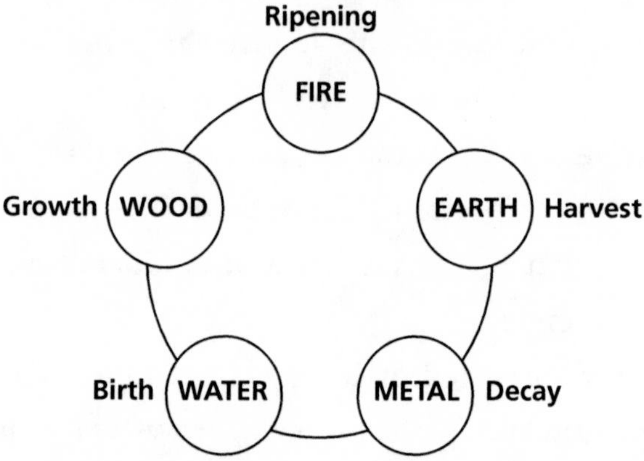

In our contemporary language, we have chosen to refer to these phases
as start-up, growth, maturation, maintenance, and evaluation.

Often in teaching these ideas to colleagues in health care, we are struck by their response to the description of the model. There is such wisdom and symmetry to the Five Element model that by the time we finish explaining the Control cycle we hear a collective "Aha!" as each person grasps the beauty of what is being described. It is almost as if we have a visceral response to the energies being described because the process matches our own experiences so closely. Water energy, with its ability to wind its way over, under, and around, reminds us of the need to be adaptable. When thinking about sap rising in the trees or

Control Cycle—

explains one of two ways the five elements or energies relate to each other. In this cycle each energy has the power to control or diminish the power of another energy. Example: Metal cuts (balances) Wood or Water puts out (balances) Fire.

buds bursting open in the spring, we recognize the energy that allows us to speak up and express a differing opinion or to head out on an adventure. The spark of Fire energy reminds us of the sparkle in a friend's eyes as the friend talks about a passion for a hobby. The image of "Mother Earth" comes to mind when we talk about friends or colleagues who exhibit the nourishing centeredness of Earth energy. Metal energy is sometimes a little more difficult to grasp until we talk about the essential minerals and precious gems at the core of the earth and then we intuitively gravitate to the importance of core values and friends we value for their rock-solid personal integrity.

Figure 1–3: Control or K'o Cycle

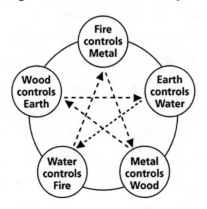

Having watched the ease with which this model can be conveyed to those who are open to its richness, we realized that in developing this ancient model the Chinese were describing laws of being in the natural world to which we can all relate. The completeness of this model is best described by Elias and Ketchum in their book, *Reclaiming the Feminine Spirit of Healing*, as they write:

> *Chinese sages and scholars devoted their energies to understanding and describing the vital life-giving connections between the universe, the earth, and the human being. Over many hundreds of years, they created an elaborate philosophy aimed at a higher awareness of the grand unit of the cosmos, with the eminently practical goal of helping people lead a healthy, happy, moral life.*[7]

As their understanding of the Five Elements or primary energies evolved, the Chinese made a number of associations between what they could see in their everyday lives and these five elements. They associated each of the elements with seasonal changes they experienced throughout the year. For example, the frozen lakes (Water) seen in the winter thaw in the spring, nourishing plants and trees (Wood). In the summer, these plants and trees blossom into bright colors (Fire). They bear ripe fruit (Earth) in the late summer. In the fall, the leaves drop off the trees (Metal) and as they degenerate they provide essential minerals for (Water) and the cycle begins again (see Figure 1-4). The Chinese also associated each of the elements with a color. Water is blue-black, Wood is green, and Fire is red. Earth energy is associated with the color yellow, for a time of

Figure 1–4: Elements and Association

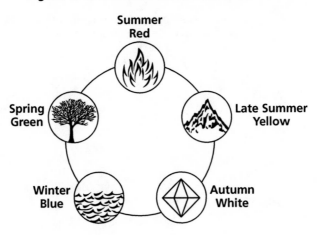

ripening, and Metal with anything metallic colored, but most often the color white.[8]

Body organs were also assigned to each of the five energies. However, these are thought of as "organ networks," not only in specific anatomical terms, but also in metaphorical terms to reflect the emotional and spiritual qualities that were associated with each of the five energies.[9]

The reason for their different view of the way organs function in the body is that Chinese culture does not separate body and soul. According to Chinese medicine, each organ has an emotional, spiritual, and mental function in addition to the physiological functions we attribute to each of the internal organs in western medicine. In Chinese medicine, one organ network is associated with each of the Five Elements except for Fire, which has two. These organ networks reflect the functions of that particular element in sustaining overall health and well-being (see Figure 1-5).

Figure 1-5: Organ Networks

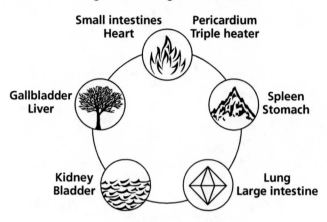

An example to illustrate this concept is in the way the Chinese associate the liver and gallbladder with the forcefulness of Wood energy. In western medicine we view the liver as an anatomical structure located in the middle, right side of the body, and we know it is responsible for removing toxins from the blood and making glucose for the body to have the fuel it needs to function properly. The Chinese view the liver as being a brilliant military strategist responsible for the smooth flow of energy and blood to every cell in the body. As the Commander with visionary qualities, the liver is responsible for making sure that the body's physical, emotional, and spiritual needs are kept in balance.

The other organ associated with Wood energy is the gallbladder. Those of us schooled in western medicine see the gallbladder as a small, pear-shaped organ that stores and distributes bile to aid in the breakdown of certain foods for digestion. The Chinese view the gallbladder as not only responsible for these functions, but as a wise Judge who, in

Organ network—

the term the Chinese give to the anatomical structures and metaphorical functions of each element (or energy) related to health and well-being. Example: Water energy is represented by the kidney and bladder.

making good decisions, is able to moderate our behavior. The spiritual quality associated with forceful Wood energy is creativity—the ability to create and bring forth something new, just as Wood energy is expressed in new growth in the spring. Since the "pushing forth" of the Commander (Wood) is likely to generate friction, the Chinese associate the emotion of anger or conflict with Wood energy.

The Five Elements and the key functions expressed as "organ networks" are listed in Table 1-1. While some of the organ networks are more easily understood than others, the important thing is to make the transition from thinking about the "organ" as we learned it in anatomy classes to understanding the metaphorical nature being depicted and the Twelve Key Functions the Chinese view as essential for maintenance of health or balance.

The first organ network associated with Fire energy is the heart and small intestine network. Its function is as the seat of consciousness, establishing interconnectedness between our internal and external life. In more traditional Chinese medicine texts, a second organ network is associated with the Fire element and is referred to as pericardium and triple heater, but has no corresponding visceral structures. Post and other authors have characterized the function of this network as integrating internal and external communication.[10] Earth energy is associated with the spleen and stomach organ network and the function is to generate and distribute nourishment. "Like a minister of agriculture overseeing production and distribution...the raw material of food and experience...is assimilated...to fuel the body and mind."[11] The organ network associated with Metal energy is lung and large intestine. Its key function is to separate out those substances no longer needed by the body, determining what is useful and useless. Water energy has associated with it the kidney and bladder organ network. Together these organ networks make up the twelve key functions necessary to maintain body functioning and this division of labor ensures that all tasks are accomplished.

* * *

While, at first glance, these associations may seem irrelevant to organizations, consider the metaphorical nature of the model to get a clearer understanding. The lung function, for example, depicts the importance of "inspiration" within the mind, body, and spirit of the individual, not just the physical inspiration accomplished by the lungs. In the phase of ending or closure, which is the phase of Metal energy, the function of "letting go" of that which is finished (large intestine) while also holding fast to values or beliefs, which are "inspirational" (lungs), allows for that phase of the cycle to be completed. Also, when a healthy balance of these functions is ignored or devalued, illness or disharmony is likely to manifest in that organ system. For example, a scattered, frenetic lifestyle (characterized as excess Fire) may result in a heart attack.

Table 1-1: The Elements and Associations

Element	Color	Season	Emotion	Motivation	Organs	Mental Function	Spiritual Quality	Archetypal Personality
Water	Blue	Winter	Fear	To Generate	Kidney Bladder	Motivate Retention	Introspection	Sage
Wood	Green	Spring	Anger	To Grow	Liver Gall bladder	Judgment Decisions	Creativity	Commander
Fire	Red	Summer	Joy	To Revitalize	Heart Small intestine Pericardium Triple Heater	Communicate Prioritize	Connection	Communicator
Earth	Yellow	Late Summer	Empathy	To Stabilize	Spleen Stomach	Transform Distribute	Centeredness	Peacemaker
Metal	White	Fall	Grief	To Evaluate	Lung Large Intestine	Inspire Eliminate	Inspiration	Philosopher

Sources: Beinfield and Korngold, *Between Heaven and Earth*, New York: 1991.
Elias and Ketchum, *In the House of the Moon*, New York: 1995.
Post, "Elements of Organization," Lecture notes, Philadelphia: 1993.

Looking at all five energies, each organ network serves a function and makes a contribution to the whole personality.[12] These associations, which correlate the energies seen in nature with the body/mind/spirit, form the basis for the practice of Chinese medicine. The beauty of this model, you will find, lies in the interdependence of the five energies—in nature, in our overall health and well-being, and in the overall good health of the organization. In the next section we also see how they work interdependently for the overall good health of a group or an organization.

When you reflect on this framework for understanding the beauty of nature and the ways in which the laws of nature are replicated in the body/mind/spirit, you will also discover the invisible energy patterns that influence us and those around us. Anthropologist Gregory Bateson refers to the Five Element model as a "pattern which connects."[13] The interaction of the Five Elements brings harmony and ensures everything is in order. This system is like a circle, which has neither a beginning nor an end.

This rich pattern is even more obvious with a careful, in-depth study of the model. Other authors have explored the many health dimensions of the model and used it to identify the best times of day when each energy is strongest and even the foods to eat to enhance each energy.[14] However, for our purpose in better understanding organizational life, we have limited our journey into Chinese medicine to the identification of the five primary energies and the associations made for each of them some five thousand years ago.

Five Element Model—Key Concepts
Chi

At this point, you might well be asking: "If this is a framework for understanding how the laws of nature play out in organizations and human relationships and determine our sense of health and well-being, how do needles and acupuncture come into the picture?" The answer lies in an understanding of a key concept in Chinese medicine—the concept of chi (pronounced chee). The Chinese call chi the "vital energy" or "life force." In Japan this life force is Ki, and in yoga it is referred to as Prana.[15] This concept is perhaps foreign to us as Westerners since we cannot see or measure chi. It is interesting to note that western medicine is the only system in the world that does not recognize a vital force, by whatever name, in human beings.

Chi—

the life energy that flows naturally throughout the body in channels, called meridians, and when in balance results in a state of health and well being.

The chi, or life force, flows naturally throughout the body in channels known as "meridians." These meridians are invisible and, for the most part, follow the paths of nerves and blood vessels. There are twelve meridians in the body (to correspond with the twelve functions just described in the organ networks) and, at certain points along these channels, needles can be used to tap into that energy flow. These channels carry the life force flow in and out of the various organs and ultimately connect all of the organs in a closed system. This is analogous to how blood flows through the body to nourish all the vital organs and sustain the overall functioning of the body systems. The Chinese believe that illness results when this life force is blocked or is excessive or deficient (not flowing as it naturally would).

The acupuncture points provide access to clear the blockage and allow the chi to flow naturally again. In the next chapter you will see how the use of specific interventions in the workplace can restore a healthy level of functioning to groups and organizations so that organizations are more effective in overall performance and provide a high quality work environment for their employees. In general, though, just as vital energy flows through each of us, chi is also recognizable when we come together in groups or as an organization.

Yin and Yang

No discussion of the concept of "life force" would be complete without also exploring another key principle in Chinese medicine: the "ebb and flow" of chi, which we refer to as yin and yang. Many Westerners immediately think of the symbol for this concept, which is increasingly common and visible in our culture (see Figure 1-6). Many believe yin and yang represent opposites or balance, yet the concept covers so much more.

Figure 1-6: Interdependence of Yin and Yang

The concept of yin and yang in the Chinese belief system is a way of seeing reality such that "every aspect of the world, material and spiritual, is made up of two opposing and at the same time interdependent forces."[16] Yin and yang is a way of describing the relationship that exists between two things rather than a judgment (as in naming the opposite) of something. In this sense yin and yang differ from the western concept of dualism. Yin and yang are opposites that form a whole and in that sense depend on each other. To grasp the concept of yin and yang, think of them as "dynamic balance."[17] Yin and yang are continuously interacting and dependent on each other.

Taking this one step further, the Chinese believe that everything in life simultaneously contains its opposite. For example, at night with darkness all around us, we do not at that moment experience the day. However, the day emerges from the night. At dawn or at dusk we experience a time of balance between the two, but one could not exist without the other nor would we say one is more important than the other. Both are invariably present. There is always some yin within yang and some yang within yin and together they are a way of describing chi energy.[18] It is a matter of shifting our thinking from an "either-or" mindset to thinking in terms of "both-and." Thus it is both good and evil, both black and white, and both male and female. "Yang represents all that is expanding, moving, growing, bright, hot, masculine, and active; while Yin refers to the forces of the dark, quiet, condensation, introversion, and all that is passive, feminine, cool, and decaying."[19] The following list of yin and yang attributes helps to illustrate these ideas (see Table 1-2).

Table 1-2: Understanding Yin/Yang

General Attributes		Body/Mind	
Yin	Yang	Yin	Yang
contraction	expansion	rest	movement
downward	upward	inhale	exhale
dark	light	instinct	intelligence
cold	heat	introversion	extroversion
moon	sun	quiet	talkative
female	male	conservative	progressive
passive	active	contemplative	reactive

Source: Eckert, *Chinese Medicine for Beginners*, Rocklin, California, 1996.

The interdependence of yin and yang aspects of energy can be seen in the simple act of breathing. The exhale is the yang aspect of breath and the inhale is the yin aspect (see Figure 1-7). The Chinese recognized this principle all around them. In every object, action or quality there are yin and yang aspects, both of which represent the whole. They noticed this in behavior as well, recognizing that there are two sides to every truth. Yin and yang aspects are also evident in relationships. In reflecting on our physical, mental, and emotional health, there needs to be a time for movement and a time for rest, a time for planning and a time for making decisions, a time to give and a time to receive.

Figure 1-7: Yin and Yang of Breathing

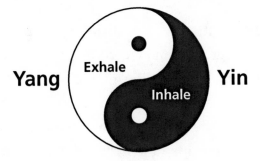

While many of us have an intellectual understanding of the concept of yin and yang (balance), its importance in maintaining our vitality (chi) is ignored in much of our culture today. We have only to examine our own lives. It is apparent in our behavior as we strive to pack more and more into each day, accepting additional responsibilities or commitments without adequate resources for carrying through on them. It is seen in our organizations as well when there is insistence on mandatory overtime for employees in order to get the work done or downsizing that leaves the "survivors" with their own work as well as the work of those who left. Often a "wake up call" in the form of an illness, a threatened divorce, high staff turnover, or an employee unionization attempt is necessary to remind us of the need for balance in sustaining ourselves or our organizations. The Five Element model helps us comprehend the "invisible forces" that influence how we live and work together and serves as a reminder of basic truths. Understanding yin and yang energy can help us honor our own common sense when our intuition tells us it is time to "regroup and refill" personally—or that we need to pay attention to the quality of work life in our organizations.

The Five Elements and Personality Types

Quite often at this point when we teach the Five Element model someone will look over the matrix listing the personality type and general nature associated with each of the energies and ask, "How can I determine which of these five energies fits me?" Another common question is, "If I feel drawn to the ocean when I need to refill, does that mean I am a Water-type person?" In groups experiencing problems in making decisions or taking a stand, someone will ask, "Do we need some more Wood types?" We tell them to remember in learning this model that it is about energy and the flow of energy in nature and all living organisms. All living systems have all of the elements present. It is not about labeling people or forcing others into categories.

If we look closely, we all can find ourselves moving in and out of these various energies in one day. We may be partially awake in the early morning and find ourselves in a reflective mood (Water) as we think over the events of the previous day. We get up to exercise and find ourselves feeling the need to stretch our limbs (Wood—no pun intended) before going into work. Perhaps we have a meeting with coworkers we really enjoy. The laughter comes easily (Fire) as we problem solve and agree on a plan to deal with an issue (Wood). We take advantage of the drive home in the late afternoon to process the events of the day and prepare to make the transition (Earth) between our work day and our home life. Watching the setting sun and preparing the evening meal, we feel a sense of closure (Metal) on another day and a time to feel gratitude for the blessings of the day. We take stock and evaluate (Metal) what has been accomplished and feel the need for sleep (Water). Sometimes we are aware of having overused a particular energy, for instance, if we have been on the telephone talking all day (Fire) and we may just want some quiet time to ourselves to reflect (Water). While we may not be conscious of these energy shifts it is obvious as we use this model that energy ebbs and flows with the events and the tasks of each day.

This having been said, it is important to note that the Chinese believe each of us is born with a special affinity for one of the five energies. Most of the time in teaching the Five Element model to members of a group who know each other well, we hear the side conversations begin as we review the archetypes for each energy and the ways that each energy manifests itself in groups. Soon the group is recognizing Mary's Earth energy as we think about how she loves to bring in homemade cookies for staff meetings, or Frank's Water energy when he quietly reflects on how a meeting is getting off track and brings the group back to the purpose for the meeting. The Five Element model offers us a deeper understanding of the "invisible energy patterns" that influence each of us in every aspect of our lives and oftentimes this understanding allows us to be more tolerant of each other and more appreciative of the diversity and talents we find in our family and friends.

Affinity for/dominant energy—

although we all exhibit aspects of each energy, the Chinese believe that each individual is born with an affinity for one of the five energies, which is the dominant energy...much like one is either more introverted or extroverted. The same can be extrapolated for groups or organizations.

For those interested in learning about their primary energy, the questionnaire developed by Elias and Ketchum in their book, *Chinese Medicine for Maximum Immunity: Understanding the Five Elemental Types for Health and Well-Being,* can help you determine which of the Five Elements you have more or less of an affinity for and perhaps some insight into your inclinations and tendencies. It is important to remember that there is no "one best energy" and that while we have an affinity for a particular energy, we move in and out of all the energies on any given day. The different roles we play as parents, friends or teachers may find us moving in and out of different energies as the situation demands. It is helpful in learning this model to focus more on recognizing and gaining an appreciation for each of the five primary energies surrounding us rather than trying to decide "who is what." The beauty of this model is in its appreciation for all of nature and the intricate patterns and connections reflected in this ancient wisdom.

As Jason Elias writes:

The Five Element system is ancient and exotic, yet it is eminently practical and accessible...Earth types need only look out the window at their gardens to understand the nourishing, stabilizing nature of their energy. If you have an affinity for Fire you feel passion and joy for life...the differences between us are not flaws that one of us has strayed from the norm, but symbols of the wonderful complexity of life. What would our world be like without rivers...mountains...woodlands, without the radiance of the sun or the reflected light of the moon? The beauty and integrity of our world depend on all the elements and each element expresses its basic nature in unique ways.[20]

Summary

In the next chapter we apply the basic tenets of the Five Element model to organizational life and the ways we function in the workplace. These Five Elements and their corresponding twelve functions can be seen in how we work through a change process or come together as a group to get work done. Having just begun this journey, hopefully we will gain insight into our natural abilities and flow with our energy rather than forcing it or fighting it. We will perhaps learn to be more tolerant of others who "march to the beat of a different drummer" and see things from a different perspective. Perhaps we will learn to listen to our bodies and honor the intuitive need for time in the woods or a walk by the ocean—trusting the small voice calling us to take time to be quiet and still. We may even decide that life can be more balanced and that there is something more than "overdrive" and "collapse." As with any journey, we never quite know where it will take us or what impressions will sink in and cause us to make more permanent changes. One thing should be obvious at this point, however: The Five Element model offers us ancient wisdom and a wonderful yet practical road map for the journey.

Applying the Model to Modern Organizational Life

Sharon Cox and Jo Manion

How can a five-thousand-year-old model help us on our journey to understanding systems and organizations today? Translating this powerful and ancient wisdom to modern times, although challenging, is easier than it seems. Surprisingly, many of the issues faced by China's early rulers are fundamentally similar to the concerns experienced by modern leaders today. According to Post:

Historically (eleventh to fifteenth century BC) the Chinese Imperial Court hired advisors to help the Emperor and his ministers achieve their peak performance individually and as a team. The "Nei Ching," the now famous Yellow Emperor's Classic of Internal Medicine, *holds countless examples of how the Emperor was helped by his chief advisor: by helping select appropriate cabinet (team) members, by advising about strategic planning...These advisors were coaches who helped intensify the effect of energy expended by the ruler himself, his court appointees, and by leaders of government divisions.*[1]

Those early consultants, trained in health maintenance as well as politics and management, believed that a healthy organization was one that could accomplish more while using less energy. This idea resonates with the admonition we hear so often today to "Work smarter, not harder." Those consultants to the emperor identified twelve key functions (as described in Chapter 1) and associated these functions with the Five Elements so that within each element or phase certain functions must be attended to if that phase is to be completed or accomplished in a balanced way. If these functions are ignored or poorly accomplished, disharmony results and we fail to function to our true capacity. To apply this wisdom in our work life, we must understand the functions in depth.

We refer to the model introduced in Chapter 1 as the Five Element/Twelve Function model to help capture the essence and symmetry of it and to see its applicability to our life in organizations. Over the following pages, as we explore this model in depth, keep in mind that the Chinese language is very metaphorical, so we advise you to think in this way to grasp the full meaning of each function and apply the concept to organizational life.

Twelve Functions in Organizational Life

The Five Element/Twelve Function model gets its richness in part from the way the system figuratively describes the interaction of energy. In Chinese medicine, primal forces and relationships all serve as a metaphorical framework or context in which to move from the microcosm of the individual to the macrocosm of the group or organization. So, just as one's individual health is dependent on the optimal functioning of the organ networks, so too the twelve key functions associated with these organ networks must be incorporated by groups or organizations seeking to function to their full capacity. These twelve functions provide a template for assessing the "healthiness" of a group or organization (see Figure 2-1).

Figure 2-1: Five Elements, Twelve Functions

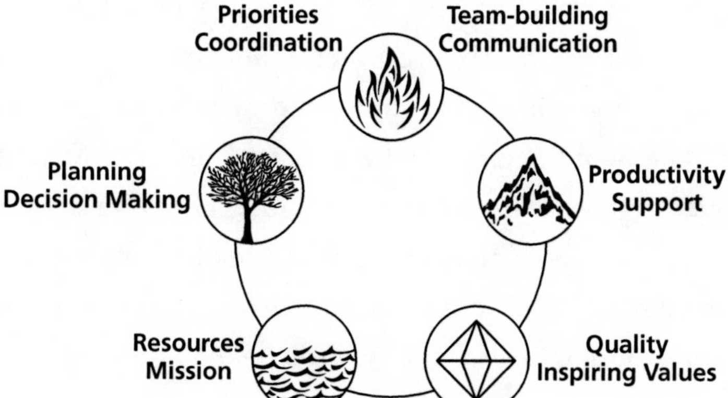

Post, N. "Elements of Organization," training program lecture notes. Philadelphia, 1993.

The Functions of Water Energy—
Resources, Mission

The Water element or phase is concerned with essence, the primal force that makes us do what we do and deals with our reason for being. In an organization, the primary issue needing attention in this phase is the "what"—what motivates us as a group and what do we have to work with in this effort? The essential task for the group that emerges is to be clear about their motivation and use of resources. In this regard it is also important to be mindful of boundaries to stay focused rather than trying to be "all things to all people." Water is most powerful when focused and flowing within boundaries, as we know. The image of a swamp is an example of water without a purposeful focus or clear and firm boundaries.

When water functions are extrapolated to the organizational level, we find a clear sense of mission and purpose as well as effective resource management. When the organization's mission is lived out rather than serving as just a "framed statement hanging by the elevator," an environment of trust can be fostered. If resources are generated and allocated appropriately, this also contributes to a climate of trust. People then believe they will have the resources required to do their work. When these functions are ignored, taken lightly or poorly executed, a fearful work environment is likely to develop.

Whether the organization fails to clarify a sense of mission or direction, or fails to live up to its clearly stated mission, the results are the same. When resources are inadequate or poorly or unfairly allocated, the results are the same. This energetic imbalance is reflected in conversational themes or phrases people use to describe their feelings. In these situations, employees may complain of a sense of "floundering" or a fear of "going under" and failing. Interestingly, these themes also emerge in group artistic drawings. When asked to draw a group picture of "how they see things in the organization today," individuals portray these imbalances in their drawings. In a group struggling with a lack of direction or trust issues, the pictures often have a water "theme." Drawings of ships sinking, islands isolated by bodies of water, sharks or monsters in the water, drowning victims, or people "jumping ship" are not at all uncommon when the group has an imbalance in Water energy.

The Functions of Wood Energy— Planning, Decision Making

The second phase, Wood energy, is concerned with "how"—how are we going to get things done? At the group level the key functions relate to taking the time to plan and to develop a mechanism and structure for decision making. These discussions typically bring up control issues and may even foster some healthy conflict as differing views are expressed and efforts are made to reach consensus. In group development, this phase has been characterized as the "storming phase" since conflict is common at this point. The measure of completing this phase is in whether or not the group can work through the conflict, make a decision, and follow through on its plan.

These same issues could be framed as a question. Does the organization have an effective structure in place for decision making and a workable vision for the future? When we raise these issues in organizations, we have often found that a myriad of committees may be in place, but the actual decisions about what really matters continue to be made at upper levels in the organizational hierarchy. Roles overlap and reporting structures are cumbersome, resulting in a perpetual storming phase that impedes healthy organizational development. However, when these functions have been given appropriate attention, a strong sense of initiative develops and people evidence a "can do" attitude. Effective systems are in place to monitor progress and encourage course corrections when undesired results occur. Dissenting opinions are valued and healthy conflict engenders better group decisions.

Leaders in organizations with a healthy balance of Wood energy are often seen as "visionary" and their work is termed "cutting edge." And visionary leadership is not limited to those people who hold line positions, but can emerge from any level of the organization. When Wood energy is deficient—or excessive—the vision may have been articulated, but those who have to make it work are unclear about next steps or time frames. Rarely will employees have participated in the development of the vision. Instead of having a shared vision, the vision is that of one individual's or one group's work that is disseminated to employees and other key stakeholders in the organization. Yet, as we know, only a shared vision has the power to gain commitment from those in the vision community.

The Functions of Fire Energy—
Priorities, Coordination,
Team Building, Communication

Fire energy is about activity and connection, when the organization's mission and resources come together with the vision and the plan to create a "go for it" spirit. Here a sense of fun, enthusiasm, and esprit de corps emerges as people enjoy their work. The key functions for groups to consider for this phase include coordination, priority setting, communication, and team building. In groups with balanced Fire energy, effective problem solving and a sense of "we are in this together" are evident. An easy laughter, teasing each other, and ability to negotiate with other groups are also characteristic of Fire energy.

Yet when these key functions fail to be addressed appropriately, the language again offers a vital clue as to the lack of balance in this energy. Typical expressions include, "We just run around and put out fires," "Everything is a front-burner issue," or "I'm just feeling fried." Information is tightly held or even withheld, and this environment often results in the formation of "cliques" at every level in the organization. These exclusive groups are problematic for any organization seeking health as they are based on excluding others in some way. Workplaces where people feel excluded are not conducive to high-quality output. Members disengage emotionally from the chaotic, dissatisfying environment and often complain of burnout.

While working recently with a management team caught up in excessive Fire energy, we noticed that not only were their words descriptive of the dominant energy, but the images they chose to depict their perceptions of the organization also reflected this energy. In response to the question, "How do you see things in your organization today?" they drew erupting volcanoes, figures sitting in the hot seat, and bodies in the frying pan jumping into the fire!

When fire energy is balanced at the organizational level attention to coordinating work efforts becomes much like that of a symphony orchestra. Efforts are made to sort multiple priorities and communicate effectively, both internally and externally, with key groups in the community. These are the organizations that are selected for honors and named on the list of "Ten best places to work." Their market position is firmly established. They also have good public relations and often are in the enviable position of choosing the best and brightest applicants in their recruitment efforts.

The Functions of Earth Energy— Productivity, Support

The season for Earth energy is late summer, a time of harvest. Metaphorically, the Earth phase describes a time to enjoy the fruits of one's labor. The pace is slower and activities are more routine and cyclical in nature. The organization has moved from the "what" to the "how," and through the fun and expansive "go for it" stage. Now the issue is maintaining productivity over time or sustaining all that has been accomplished in the earlier phases. The group functions in the Earth phase relate to stability and productivity. Critical questions include: "Do people have what they need to get their job done, and can their efforts be sustained? Do group members feel supported and cared about in meaningful ways rather than feeling like just 'a pair of hands on the project'?" Easily maintained routines are established that result in high productivity.

Another critical question is concerned with outcomes. "Did all our 'busyness' (Fire) lead to anything worthwhile?" When Earth functions are overlooked too few or ineffective systems are in place and productivity is poor. Employees often feel as if they are going in circles and making no progress. There is a sense of "being stuck" that is characteristic of an imbalance in Earth energy.

Energy imbalance—

state of the human system when there is too little (deficiency) or too much (excess) of a single or multiple energies. Interventions are directed to replenishing deficient energies or balancing the excess energy to regain a state of health.

At the organizational level, functions in this phase relate to production and support services. Do projects actually come to fruition and are operations run smoothly? Is there a sense of order and harmony within? Are internal and external customers satisfied with services and is there a sense of pride in the workforce? In this phase the group or organization reaps what has or has not been accomplished in the earlier phases. If the tasks of earlier phases have been accomplished and all issues related to the key functions are attended to, the benefits are apparent.

But when Earth energy is seriously out of balance in an organization, absenteeism and illness rates are high. Employees sometimes feel that management is not attending to their needs for support or that processes needed for productivity are not in place. Language again reflects the imbalance in energy when employees complain, "It feels like I am carrying the weight of the world" or, "I feel off-center." Sometimes the words bring images of being stuck, with phrases like, "It feels like we are treading through quicksand." Staff nurses and other caregivers are particularly frustrated with broken systems and often voice complaints, such as, "Whenever I go to care for the patient I have to spend time tracking down all the equipment and supplies ahead of time—I never have what I need to complete a task." The essential question needing attention is, "Are we being productive or just busy?" The answer to that question often reflects the quality of Earth energy in an organization.

The Functions of Metal Energy— Quality, Evaluation

The focus of metal energy is on completion. Based on values and standards the group must undertake an evaluation of its effectiveness and let go of what is not working. The shared values and belief in high standards provide the inspiration for this effort.

Norms of behavior and ethical standards are also a factor. The value of individual contributions is recognized and rewarded. When groups fail in this phase, though, letting go becomes difficult and impedes progress. This is often referred to as "carrying around old baggage."

If values and standards are taken only superficially, a lack of meaning or demoralization is evident in the group. Too often organizations establish their core values because it is the current touted management practice. Standards may be established primarily to comply with regulatory agencies. If the organization fails to live up to these values and standards, the incongruity is quickly apparent to employees and organizational commitment diminishes. Not surprisingly, this is often experienced when an organization faces difficult financial challenges.

Organizations that state, "People are our most important asset," and yet undertake involuntary downsizing without exploring other avenues of reducing expenses are a good example. Downsizing may be necessary but it must be handled in an ethical way congruent with the organization's stated values or employees can experience a significant sense of loss. In one organization, a decision was made to require all employees to reapply for their positions and for some positions to be eliminated. A stated core value of the organization was competence, yet the primary deciding factor for employees to be reinstated was based on tenure. Even though this discrepancy was identified, nothing was done to change the decision-making factors in this case.

At the organizational level healthy Metal energy is evident when there is true commitment to quality, not just lip service. In other words, continuous quality improvement describes the way work is accomplished in the organization; it is not "just a program." Systems for performance evaluation are in place and the reward system is equitable and positive, reinforcing performance for actions that strengthen the organization and its service or product. Ethical standards are upheld and personal integrity is valued. The leadership inspires confidence and "walk their talk."

With metal energy in balance, the organization attends to the need for closure and provides farewell parties or retirement dinners to recognize contributions of the staff. Attention to aesthetics is another characteristic of healthy Metal energy, evident in organizations with artwork and sculpture on display or who have a quiet chapel for reflection attending to the spiritual needs of both employees and clients. The physical environment of the workplace is pleasing and inviting. Attending to issues of quality and value-based practice, while also effectively eliminating non-value-added activities, prepares the way to revisit the mission and purpose and begin the cycle again (see Figure 2-1).

The Five Element Functions in Summary

Given the logical sequence of these twelve functions and the way they naturally build one on the other, one might think that these issues and needs of the organization would automatically come to mind and be actual routine considerations for groups or organizations that want to achieve high-quality products or outcomes. All too often, however, we see individuals, groups or even major corporations ignore the wisdom in this model. A good example is the manufacturing industry. Start-up companies are often so intent on growing (Wood) and selling their products in ever-expanding markets (Fire) that they may lose sight of their capacity to deliver on all those orders (Earth) and, in the scramble, product quality suffers (Metal).

In any organization, groups of individuals also easily get caught up in this same cycle. They begin with enthusiasm and commitment. They have a multitude of meetings and create lots of activity (Fire), but fail to achieve any real outcomes or closure (Earth and Metal). Yet, when closely examined, successful people, groups, and organizations have somehow dealt with all of these functions. They have learned from experience and can grasp intuitively key elements to consider in approaching any task. We are convinced that this is a partial explanation for why there is such resonance with this model when it is explained to audiences. The positive response to the model is validation of the approach used by the Chinese over the millennia. Successful people recognize it because they have been using these approaches in their own practice.

The Five Element/Twelve Function model provides us a framework from which to see our patterns and learn from our experience. Dr. Nancy Post and her colleagues who were trained in acupuncture as well as group dynamics observed hundreds of groups and developed a framework for applying the Five Element Model in groups or organizations. The key issues inherent in work life are organized by element in this model (see Figure 2-2). Post coined the term "Systems Energetics" to describe this template.[2]

Figure 2-2: Developmental Issues by Element

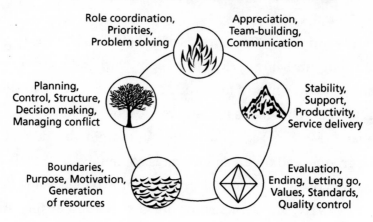

Role coordination, Priorities, Problem solving

Appreciation, Team-building, Communication

Planning, Control, Structure, Decision making, Managing conflict

Stability, Support, Productivity, Service delivery

Boundaries, Purpose, Motivation, Generation of resources

Evaluation, Ending, Letting go, Values, Standards, Quality control

Source: Post, N. and W. Bellows, "The Principles of Systems Energetics," training program, San Francisco, 1988.

3

Organizing Principles

Sharon Cox and Jo Manion

The application of the Five Element/Twelve Function model to the workplace is relatively simple if we grasp the concepts and organizing principles that can be extrapolated from the model. It is these principles that today make this timeless model come alive and provide insights into ways to deal with the realities of our work life in the twenty-first century.

As you reflect on the beauty and symmetry of the Five Element/Twelve Function model, as described in these first chapters, keep in mind a few simple truths that need to be reemphasized. While these may seem overly simplistic, even patently obvious, the reality is that these principles are often forgotten or left unnoticed as we go about our work.

Principle #1: Energy flows naturally. The vital energy or chi in any system flows naturally from one element to another unless an energy imbalance blocks the natural flow.

Principle #2: The Creation (Shen) cycle reflects the natural, developmental flow of energy and the interdependence of each of the five phases for optimal functioning.

Principle #3: The Control (K'o) cycle reflects the ways in which excessive energy can be controlled and brought back into balance.

Principle #4: Each energy has two aspects that need to be balanced for optimal functioning (referred to as the Yin/Yang Juncture).

Principle #5: To maintain balance one must attend to both using (expending) and restoring (replenishing) energy.

Principle #6: Each system has a unique blend of energy and an affinity for a specific energy. Each individual is born with a natural affinity for a particular energy and will manifest an archetypal personality associated with that energy.

In the chapters that follow we highlight ways in which these principles are either followed or violated in our everyday experiences in groups and organizations. It becomes increasingly clear that the basic principles from the emperor's court of ancient China still have relevance for us today.

Energy blocked—

a disruption of the natural flow of an energy. When energy is blocked, there is a loss of health or effectiveness.

Principle # 1: Energy flows naturally.

The vital energy or chi in any system flows naturally from one element to another unless an energy imbalance blocks the natural flow. As mentioned earlier, energy cannot be forced. And, when a system is healthy, the energy flows without outside intervention. This principle leads to an operating guideline, which appears in later chapters, referred to as the "Law of Least Action." Basically it states that when energy is blocked or not flowing normally, selected interventions should begin with the least action possible. For our purposes, an intervention is defined as a purposeful act to improve or modify a situation or condition existing in a group or organization. Using the Law of Least Action, we see right away whether the intervention is effective because the energy begins moving again and outcomes are effective.

Figure 3-1: Five Elements as Change Process

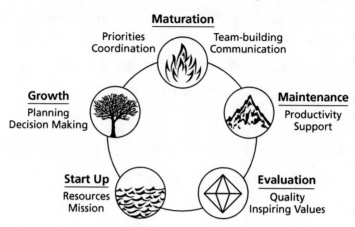

Maturation

Priorities
Coordination

Team-building
Communication

Growth

Planning
Decision Making

Maintenance

Productivity
Support

Start Up

Resources
Mission

Evaluation

Quality
Inspiring Values

Principle # 2: The Creation (Shen) cycle reflects the natural, developmental flow of energy and the inter-dependence of each of the five phases for optimal functioning.

The natural flow of energy in a balanced way is apparent as we observe the change of seasons. As we say, there is a time for each season and we would not think of rushing one season to get to another or, for that matter, skipping a season to get to another. Even though we may be impatient for spring after an especially harsh winter, we say to ourselves, change takes time. In our workplaces we see this patience reflected in a well-managed change process (see Figure 3-1). We take the time to develop a clear sense of purpose and make sure we have the resources needed to start the process, which is attending to the start-up phase of Water energy. As the project grows (Wood phase), we take the time to plan and reach consensus on key decisions with a structure put in place to foster input from stakeholders and ensure consistency of decisions. As the process gains momentum and moves into full swing, it expands to involve different groups of people (Fire). At this point we need to focus on priorities, coordination, communication, and team building so that the right hand knows what the left hand is doing. We make sure that people have what they need to sustain the change effort (Earth), whether this is time for meetings, up-to-date equipment or the most current software. We make every effort to be productive by creating efficient systems and processes and measuring outcomes to track our progress. Finally, in the Metal phase, we take the time to evaluate the effectiveness of the change to determine if quality outcomes were achieved and we use data collected to make necessary adjustments and let go of what is not working.

Intervention—

the process of applying the wisdom of the Five Element Model to work/life situations to effect a desired outcome.

However natural and obvious this sequence of events might seem, all of us have experienced change processes in which this sequence was not honored. We have rushed through or even ignored the mission/resources stage and have been told to just get it done! We have started many projects but often did not take the time to come full circle, and attend to outcomes and an honest and critical evaluation of results. When this evaluative stage is omitted, we are doomed to repeatedly make the same mistakes. In teaching this approach to change, which is as natural as the changing of the seasons, often someone will say, "This may be natural and logical, but we seldom do it this way." In Chapter 10 we explore more uses of the Five Element/Twelve Function model as it relates to organizational change.

The natural flow of energy is also evident when we watch how groups come together to accomplish their work. Assuming that everyone plays their part and takes ownership for the outcomes achieved, the group is seen as performing well and is in balance. However, we have all experienced groups where one person (perhaps with strong Wood energy) takes over and dominates the group. Instead of everyone accepting ownership, it is as if they defer to this take-charge style (excess Wood) and the spokesperson assumes a disproportionate leadership role while others choose to swallow how they really feel. The Chinese would say that the spokesperson has altered the natural flow of Wood energy in the group. As other group members fail to speak up in deference to this spokesperson, the natural give and take of ideas is blocked. This blockage (more fully discussed in Chapter 9) eventually causes a disruption or disharmony if left unattended. Perhaps this disruption in the natural flow of energy would be more recognizable if we were cognizant of the Cycle of Creation and the natural flow of energy in a healthy system.

Principle # 3: The Control (K'o) cycle reflects the ways in which excessive energy can be controlled and brought back into balance.

The beauty and power of the Control cycle is that it can be used to bring us back into balance and optimal functioning (see Figure 3-2). However, the use of this key principle is dependent upon the recognition that we are out of balance. The K'o cycle reminds us that while the five phases naturally support each other, as just described in the Creation cycle, they also serve to control each other if an energy is excessive and out of balance. Taking time in the middle of a hectic day (Fire) to sit quietly in the office with the door shut to collect one's thoughts and reflect (Water) on what really needs to get done and what could wait until the next day is an example. This simple intervention uses Water energy to balance excessive Fire and restores a sense of equilibrium. All too often, however, we fail to notice how rushed we have been feeling all day. Finally, by evening we change gears and collapse on the sofa after dinner, depleted of vital energy.

Figure 3-2: Control or K'o Cycle

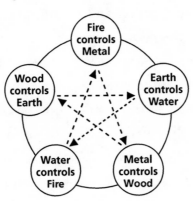

In groups that are struggling and out of balance, conflict issues and disagreements on how something needs to be done are evident. The group's discussions become more heated, with members polarized into opposing factions. While some conflict is useful, this kind of splintering into rival alliances indicates an imbalance in Wood energy. Reviewing the Control (K'o) cycle reminds us that Metal balances Wood. We could take time out from the heated discussions to set up a way to evaluate each of the options under discussion (Metal) and use this data to make decisions. In this example, Metal energy balances Wood energy so that better decisions are made. Metal energy can also be used to balance contentious Wood energy by calling for an issue to be tabled until the next meeting, which brings closure (Metal) to discussion and often allows for cooler heads to prevail.

A prevailing culture of entitlement is another imbalance that is common in health care organizations. Entitlement occurs when employees are comfortable and believe there is little likelihood that they could lose their jobs. This attitude is especially prevalent in the midst of today's workforce shortages. It results in an attitude of, "Well, they won't get rid of me, there are too few of us available." In many of our organizations, excess Earth energy results in supporting and nurturing employees beyond their point of effectiveness. People are supported regardless of substandard or inadequate performance. Using the K'o cycle and this principle of controlling energy, the appropriate intervention becomes clear. Wood energy is mobilized. Roles and expectations are clearly defined and performance contracts established. Deviations from performance are noted and discussed, and these form the basis of appropriate consequences.

Principle #4: Each energy has two aspects that need to be balanced for optimal functioning.

Much of our discussion of the Five Element/Twelve Function model has been to illustrate how the different elements support or balance each other, their interdependence. The principle of yin and yang relates to the relationships of energy within the element itself. The Chinese believe that for optimal functioning of an element, both the yin and yang aspects of that element need to be in dynamic balance. If the element is not functioning well because yin and yang aspects are out of balance, the energy is blocked and does not naturally flow to the next element in the Creation (Shen) cycle.[1]

An example to illustrate this principle is apparent when examining the nature of Wood energy as it is manifested in many organizations. As mentioned earlier, Wood energy has two functions, planning and decision making. The yin aspect is planning and the yang aspect is decision making (see Figure 3-3). These two aspects are out of balance when we pay more attention to one than the other or actually neglect one for the other. This occurs in organizations when planning meetings go on endlessly and never culminate in a decision. The imbalance in the other direction occurs when we make knee-jerk decisions without taking the time to thoughtfully consider a workable implementation plan. In both examples, the yin and yang of Wood is out of balance and disharmony is experienced in the system. An example from Water energy is becoming more prevalent today. In some organizations the stated mission is far more grandiose than can be achieved with their available resources.

Figure 3-3: Yin and Yang in Each Element

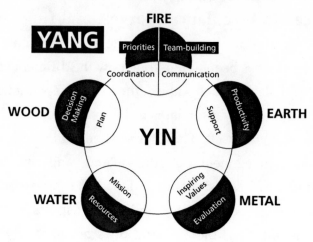

Figure 3-3 sorts the Twelve Functions associated with the Five Elements as either yin or yang aspects. Optimal functioning of a group or organization is achieved by keeping the yin and yang aspects balanced.[2]

On the outside of the circle, the functions represented are those of yang-type energy. Resource allocation, decision making, priorities, team-building systems for productivity and quality evaluation all require a more outward-going, aggressive approach intended to boldly achieve results. The inner circle functions are the more receptive, quiet, and passive energy reflective of yin-type energy. These functions include developing missions, planning, coordinating, communication, supporting and inspiring values.

These yin functions are often referred to as the "soft" side of management. Unfortunately, soft is translated in many organizations to superfluous fluff, or nice-to-do, but not essential. Organizations that fail to attend to yin energy are significantly less adept at replenishing energy, and managers find themselves wondering why their profits and market share are falling, their people are leaving in droves, and productivity levels are not what they were previously.

Balance is given great importance in healthy organizations and systems and it is demonstrated in several ways. Expending energy is balanced with replenishing energy. Time and attention is paid to implementing change and anchoring change. Reflecting on the purpose is balanced with carrying it out. Reward and recognition systems for the people who make the organization successful get as much attention as the public relations campaign to tell the public about itself. Being clear about our true values receives as much focus as formulating policies and procedures that tell people what to do. All of these functions are critical and any absence leads to imbalance and disharmony.

Principle # 5: To maintain balance one must attend to both using (expending) and restoring (replenishing) energy.

This principle is also related to the concept of yin and yang, reflecting the need for balancing the energies of expenditure (Wood and Fire) with the energies associated with replenishment (Earth, Metal, and Water) (see Figure 3-4).[3] In recent years we have come to recognize and accept the importance of conserving our natural sources of energy on this planet. For many years, sources of natural energy were exploited and consumed as if supplies were infinite. Almost too late, we discovered that there is a limit to the natural energy resources available and today we are more conscious of the need for cautious usage and conservation.

Figure 3-4: Expenditure and Replenishment Cycle

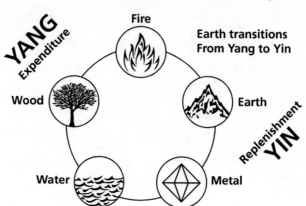

In our organizations and in our personal lives we have treated the resource of human energy in much the same way. Human energy has been exploited and treated as if it could never be fully and irrevocably depleted. We push ourselves, trying to cram more and more into our busy lives, never quite satisfied that we have accomplished enough. This principle reminds us of a basic truth we all know from experience: a healthy individual or organization simply cannot exist without understanding and capitalizing on both yin and yang energy. In other words, to maintain a healthy balance one must replenish energy in the same ratio in which energy has been used or depleted. Any human system, whether individual, group, or organizational, must be equally adept at these two types of energy.

* * *

The concepts of expenditure and replenishment in this energy model are applied broadly and need to be considered from an individual's view of what gives energy, what drains energy. Some fortunate people find their work, or some

Expenditure and Replenishment—

a key concept in maintaining health and well-being. According to this law, in a healthy system energy is used (expended) and then proportionally refilled (or replenished). Just as we are healthy when we work and play, we are in a state of health when we intentionally replenish the energies we expend.

portions of it, to be more rejuvenating than draining. Some specific aspects of work may drain our energy while other aspects replenish energy. While one person finds comfort and enjoyment in repetitive, highly structured, and detailed tasks, another might find these particularly draining. For some, relating to other people and working interdependently on projects creates an excitement and enthusiasm for the work while for others the need to relate is absolutely exhausting. Maintaining good health requires a personal understanding of what uses energy and how energy can be replenished. When expenditure and replenishment occur as a one-to-one ratio, the highest level of health is attained.

Principle #6: Each system has a unique blend of energy and an affinity for a specific energy.

Just as each individual has an affinity for a particular element or energy, the same holds true for groups and organizations and is reflected in their culture. For instance, the military is archetypal Wood energy. Structure, decision making, strategic planning, and protocols typify the culture. Health care organizations, which focus on caring, supporting, and nurturing (some would say to the point of entitlement), function predominately in Earth energy. Advertising agencies thrive on Wood and Fire energy, with the push to maximize creativity and marketing. Businesses, which emphasize total quality management as a means to improve productivity, are primarily functioning in Earth and Metal energies.

While it is important not to stereotype or categorize people with the insights gained from the Five Element/Twelve Function model, it is also important to notice dominant energies. These can be the basis for an organizational culture. These can reflect the personality of the organization and the ways to best work with that predominant energy. For instance, in a group of military officers, one would be more successful suggesting protocols be developed to deal with a situation than suggesting that a focus group to brainstorm options be formed, and then make a proposal for handling a given situation.

An awareness of the predominant energy in a group or an organization is just as useful as knowing how best to work with a certain type of individual's personality. Forming a focus group to brainstorm ideas would be an ideal approach when working in a highly creative, entrepreneurial team of computer programmers since the computer industry is archetypal Fire energy. Paying attention to these cultural cues can increase chances for success at all levels.

Archetypal personality—
the individual who manifests the classic attributes of a given energy. In the example of Fire energy, we would see an individual who is enthusiastic, good humored, excitable; who does not stand still; and who is very creative. Robin Williams is an archetypal personality for Fire energy as exemplified by his classic comedy routines.

Summary

These key principles extrapolated from the Five Element/Twelve Function model provide the basis for applying this model in organizations.[4] They are the frame of reference for understanding any number of group dynamics or problem situations as well as how to be more successful in a particular work culture.

We have been comparing the learning of this model to a journey and the principles described in this chapter can serve as a road map. These key principles provide guidance and direction in the case studies used in subsequent chapters. Our next step is to examine each of the five energies and twelve functions more closely so that our understanding is deepened and more than merely intellectual. We will use case studies and examples to illustrate the model as we proceed. But we are taking the time in our journey to get the lay of the land.

4

Water— Beginning the Cycle

Diane Miller

I stand in the presence of the sea
Heaving and rolling
Glistening and reflective,
Its sound magnetic,
I am taken to dreams as I listen.

I find the sea's mark on the sand,
Intermingled with trails of those
who emerged from its depth.
Inhaling deep breaths of its spray
I feel steadied, supported and refreshed...

Many references for Water can be found in nature: a babbling brook, morning fog, waves breaking against the shore, a frozen pond in a snow-covered park, a soft all-day rain, and dew gently pressed on a spider web now glistening in the morning sunlight.

Water, in human systems, is reflected in depth, stillness, and listening. It has a refreshing and reinvigorating quality—like a brief mid-afternoon shower or a quiet stream rolling over smoothed rocks. It is emphasis—the punctuation point in an interaction. And it is the quieter member of the group who willingly yields center stage to and is often overlooked by the extroverted Fire element.

Water, in its healthiest state, is a serene yet powerful force. It has a rhythm, a cycle. It is flexible, taking on the shape of anything containing it. An appropriate and common expression is "going with the flow." Water is adaptive, accommodating, yielding, inclusive, and fluid. It is supportive. One who is troubled often seeks out the sympathetic listening of Water energy. This listener hears the words and underlying emotions, maintains steady eye contact, and considers both sides of the issue. Water calms the excited, relaxes the overworked, and helps the emotionally confused untangle the confusion. It is a good antidote for those out of touch with feelings and the guide for getting abandoned projects back on track.

The season of Water energy is winter (see Table 4-1). It begins a new cycle. It is a time of generating and reenergizing. Winter provides a time to consider what has been accomplished, anchors what is the past, and mobilizes energy for future directions.[1] Looking out the window at a recent snowfall, things seem clean, focused, and tempting. One can hardly wait to make the first footprint on a path. But wait, says Water energy, let us first take stock of what is needed to venture out into the cold.

Table 4-1: Water Energy—Overview

Season	Winter
Color	Blue or Back
Voice	Groan
Emotion	Fear
Organs	Kidney, Bladder
Motivation	To emphasize
Thought Process	Reflective
Personality Type	Sage

Just as the liver is viewed by the Chinese as the Commander, or military strategist, the kidneys and bladder are the officials of Water that do the energetic work. They excel through their ability and cleverness. While taking in massive amounts, these officials filter, purify, store, and then eliminate. They are the gateway between the digestive and vascular system of the body. If the gateway becomes inflexible, too open or closed, disease is created. If the kidneys fail to work, there is system stress and poisoning. Water imbalances are noted by lethargy, anxiety, depression, lack of acuity of perception, and/or wishy washy behavior.[2] Feeling overwhelmed, experiencing blocked flow of thoughts or ideas, and fearing change are other signs of imbalance (see Table 4-2).

Water is represented in colors of blue or black and in expressions like the "deep blue sea" and "feeling blue." When there is an imbalance of Water element, the face takes on a blue hue, especially around the eyes and mouth.

Table 4-2: Water Energy—Work Group/Organizational Life

Characteristics Indicating Balance	Characteristics Indicating Imbalance
Introspection	Lethargy, depression Anxiety, overwhelmed Fear of change Hypercritical
Visionary	Lack of motivation and direction
Thoughtful and deep analysis	Mistrust
Firm grasp on the course	Misused or chronically misused resources
Clear about limitations	Low energy
Maintain directions with purposeful directions	Lack of boundaries

In Table 4-2, column one represents behaviors that indicate a healthy balance of water energy while column two represents unhealthy or imbalanced water energy.

Appreciating Water as part of the Five Energy system is important, using the Shen and Control cycles. Water is the child of Metal and the mother of Wood. It controls Fire. When in excess, it is controlled by Earth energy. Metal can be a source if Water is depleted (see Figures 4-1 and 4-2).

Figure 4-1: Shen Cycle

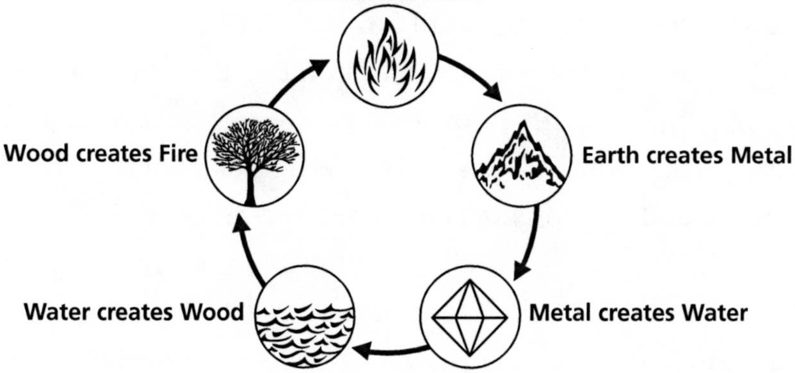

Fire creates Earth

Wood creates Fire

Earth creates Metal

Water creates Wood

Metal creates Water

Figure 4-2: Control or K'o Cycle

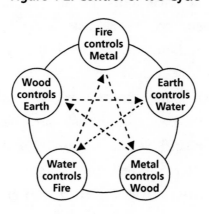

Fire controls Metal

Wood controls Earth

Earth controls Water

Water controls Fire

Metal controls Wood

Water is associated with the timeframe between 3 p.m. and 7 p.m.[3] It is noted in a salty taste in the mouth. Its sense organs are the ears and it can be heard as a groan in the voice. Considering Water in an organizational context reveals its connection with Metal and Wood energy. When coupled with the critical evaluation qualities and the capacity to let go provided by Metal, the bedrock is laid for effective future endeavors. It is the precursor to the planning, decision making, structuring, and visioning in a project—all functions of Wood energy.

Water is the preparation period at the beginning of a change cycle. A time for taking stock—assessment is an appropriate word to describe a Water attribute. Here the purpose and mission are considered and articulated. This is a time of clarifying responsibilities and the power or authority that is available to the group. It is the gathering, managing, regulating, and allocating of resources. At the beginning of a change cycle, it is very common to see Water manifestations in the fear encountered in the numerous questions about motivation and the uncertainty around support of the project. The need for reassurance is very clear. When Water is contained within appropriate boundaries, it is at its highest power and greatest effectiveness. A clear sense of direction ensues and the catalyst for change is mobilized. A project team that attends to Water energy at the beginning of its work goes on to be more persistent and self sufficient, and is not intimidated by adverse situations encountered. The team's ability to regroup and redirect as necessary evolves if the members are attentive in the early or preparation phase. Healthy Water provides a base for travel into the future.

Case Study

I worked with this particular group over a period of fifteen months. The members' responsibilities in the organization were to attend to its fiscal soundness and growth (fiduciary role), develop plans to increase market share (marketing role), and meet customers' needs (quality role). This organization enjoyed a positive and highly visible national reputation. All group members were prepared at the master or doctorate level of education.

One third of the group I worked with was centrally located geographically with the remainder of the group in offices off site. The whole group met together quarterly for retreats, where much attention was given to the setting and socializing between group members. In the periods between retreats, correspondence between members was project focused and done primarily through electronic media. Actual contact between members was limited to retreat events.

A growing number of conflicts was experienced within the group. A group of naysayers emerged and were credited with "increasing tension within the group," "slowing down the team," and "making it difficult to meet work targets." In the past year, team members had expressed a lack of confidence in the CEO and the organization was being challenged legally on some of its activities. Team members reported feeling overwhelmed. Eventually several members stepped forward to assume the role of the contract team to negotiate a service relationship with me.

Energy Assessment

I received introductory information about this team in a series of six calls, each involving a conference call with a different configuration of the contract team. On two occasions, the call was followed by a one on one call with a member who wanted to share additional background and to provide personal "concerns that I would rather not have others hear." On a number of occasions when I posed questions, members said, "We'll have to check on that," indicating there was yet another member of the contract team with different authority, and that the members of this group were unclear on their authority or lacked key information.

I eventually ascertained that the client's primary concern was centered on conflicts within the group and thus the specific need was a team-building session. I was given the authority to set the agenda and told to be ready to "meet a dysfunctional group." A small portion of my work with this group is shared here.

Since I was planning to engage in a conversation about team development, I arrived for the session at the appointed time and found the group had not progressed through their earlier morning agenda and indicated to me that they wanted to cancel my work for that day. The substance of my first interaction with the group then was limited to listening to the continuance of their discussions from the morning. They ended the meeting stating, "We aren't sure where to go next or what we need to do," and asked me to join them at a point "down the road." The accomplishment that day was their commitment to completing a team survey I would develop to provide assessment information for future work. They requested specifically that names not be associated with any information gleaned from the survey.

I developed the survey based on the Five Element/Twelve Function model and distributed a copy to each member, who returned it prior to our second session. We scheduled this session for a full day of sharing survey results and basic information on team development. The CEO selected the hotel and room for the session, a four-star hotel with an impressive environment and services. Interestingly, the room had an upper and lower tier. Six tables were randomly arranged across the two tiers seating the twenty-five members present. Unfortunately, the room was dimly lit and felt congested.

When I asked for opening feedback on the agenda, no one offered additions, comments, advice or changes. The survey completed by group members revealed:

- A lack of agreed-upon ground rules for meetings, agenda that were historically "too ambitious," with many items carried over, and timelines chronically extended (Wood)
- No clear and/or shared expectations (Water)
- Ongoing questions about responsibility and authority (Water)
- Unclear decision making and problem-solving processing (Wood)
- Task orientation to agendas with low evaluation, reflection, and limited accountability (Metal)
- "Moving targets" without clear, governing purpose and boundaries (Water)

- Continued inability to meet established plans, objectives, and target (Wood)
- Greater emphasis on performance than on team relationships and critical thinking (Fire)
- Difficulties managing resources, frequently over-spending established limits, and neglecting resources currently available within the organization (Water)
- A general lack of motivation in the membership (Water)
- Fear and lack of trust between members (Water)
- Perceived "secrecy among some members," and a resultant failure to share their knowledge and expertise with others (Water)
- Failure to celebrate and bring things to a close (Metal)

After sharing the survey information, I asked members for their comments. Several immediately pulled back in their chairs, others assumed a slumped posture, and most eyes were downcast or directed to me only (Water). A quiet comment or two was shared initially. Two members began to review individual survey questions. They asked about the basis of the questions and suggested different ways to pose the questions (Metal). One member felt the results were "depressing." Another added, "We really are a dysfunctional group, aren't we?" Then, another member stated her concern about that specific comment, saying, "I don't like stereotyping" (Water). A short discussion ensued about whether it would be beneficial to simply move on with the remainder of the agenda and reserve further comments to later in the day.

Questions and concerns were raised by members including: additional information might be needed to draw conclusions about their team's effectiveness; need to redo the survey with a specific team project in mind; and a fear that the lack of anonymity limited honest comments. Statements shared were individual and isolated in nature rather than building on previous comments. Feelings shared by members included anger "that we have gotten to this point" (Wood), "gratitude that we have this day together to get started" (Metal), and shared concern about the issues at hand (Earth).

In my assessment, I was able to see the interconnection of all five elements in this system, but noted a preponderance of evidence relating to an imbalance of the Water. The specific signs include:

Complaints: Auditory difficulty, lack of perceptual acuity, arthritic problems, cold hands and feet, lack of flow of ideas, feelings of being overwhelmed or inundated, depression, dry mouth, overreacting, lack of trust

Color: Blue or black around the mouth

Emotion: Fear

Voice: Groan or moaning

Posture: Slumped, lethargic, apathetic

Assessment of My Own Energy

Two fundamental principles should be adhered to when using the Five Element model in determining the states of energy balance and imbalance. The first is to complete a detailed, systematic assessment of the individual or group, as detailed above. An additional, critical step is to identify both the impact of the noted energy on you, the observer, and also the impact of your energy on those observed.

The mere presence of the observer will in some way affect the group. Your effectiveness is diminished or lost when this fact is overlooked. Prior to planning and carrying out an energetic intervention, you must clearly sort your energy from the energy of the group. The key cycle to practice when working with energy is: assess the group, assess and adjust self, reassess the group, and intervene. This helps you avoid the trap of either acting out your own energy issues or basing interventions on the effects the group has on you. Jumping to conclusions, stubbornly staying with an initial diagnosis, and rejecting any ideas or manifestations that might suggest another energetic finding are not operating within assessment parameters beneficial to the group.

In this case, in the second meeting with the group, given the information I received from the contract team, I needed to consciously attend to approaching the group in a non-biased way.

To do so, I reviewed the Five Element Model during the trip to the organization and paid particular attention to the key indicators of all five elements. My dual goal for the session was to establish an interaction where I would support the group's learning and also learn about the group. By holding myself in a teacher learner role rather than an expert consultant role, I was more likely to hold myself in a balanced interaction.

To further support this approach, I made a conscious decision to suspend any judgments of the group, and instead committed myself to taking in all data that emerged. Paying attention to my physical status was important. I was well rested, had avoided caffeine prior to and during the session, and made sure I was properly hydrated. I ate a light meal before the session. During the session, I avoided sitting with the group during break time to keep an objective distance and maintained the process of validating or checking with the group at regular intervals to increase the accuracy of my assessment.

Interventions

Findings from the survey provided me with a number of signals suggesting that a Water imbalance existed with an associated impact on other energies. I supplemented these findings with assessment data available during our time together and also during the initial calls to create a contractual relationship. I drew up a list of major themes and associated symptoms found in this team that indicated a Water imbalance.

- An amorphous configuration: such as continued variability in who was available for telephone conference calls, and seating that was arranged over two tiers and scattered randomly
- Submerged energy: for example, difficult to draw members into the discussion, tendency to be quiet
- Prolonged noncommittal behaviors: for example, difficulty in coming to contract terms, canceling the first scheduled work session, withholding feedback during the session
- Maintenance of secrecy: for example, a series of separate phone calls in the initial period, insistence on anonymity in the survey, discomfort with the

sharing of findings and negative reactions to findings

- Critical comments and general fussiness about the process used for assessment, the way questions were posed, the need to understand every detail
- Pessimism and feelings of despair when results were shared and in the use of negative labels like "dysfunctional group"
- Hesitancy to interact with others in the group despite repeated open urgings to do so
- Fear of assertion in developing a substantive plan and goals, difficulty identifying feelings and needs during the session

I learned right away that they would not engage in setting specific goals as a large group. I asked them to break into small teams for a fifteen minute discussion focusing on the statement: "The things I appreciate most about this team are_____" (Metal). Their themes were then to be transferred to a flip chart in picture form over a period of fifteen minutes. When individuals who questioned their own drawing skills raised their concerns, I told them to trust their creativity. In the process, I supplied the group with resources and clear boundaries for their work together (Water). Each small group was then asked to show and explain their pictures.

The discussion required members to share their thoughts and was anchored in reflection. The reference was the past and was strictly bounded in time and clear expectations. I was using a Water intervention that is supported by an evaluative component (Metal). Requiring that they present their ideas in pictures provided members with an alternative to verbally sharing thoughts. Also, at least some degree of anonymity was offered, which was needed for a sense of security.

The group completed their discussion and the resulting pictures became a foundation for moving forward on this day. The pictures were very well done and contained a variety of themes. Some common themes were identified and captured by me on a flip chart during the reports by the teams. I followed up this exercise with the request that the small teams develop yet another picture, capturing "things that could assure positive future experiences." We used the same timelines, process, and resources. This Metal to Water intervention resulted in a set of actions they could take, including:

- Developing clear purpose and expectations within the group
- Building trust
- Seeking future opportunities to celebrate what is working while focusing on future issues
- Developing truthfulness without fear of criticism
- Building knowledge, effectiveness, and positive team relationships

Our remaining group time was spent on and anchored by these themes. I concentrated on the team's overall development and used opportunities to validate their work from these two activities. At the end of our time, I introduced several of the fundamental considerations and processes for future movement of this group.

Lessons Learned

Two aspects emerged as most significant in my early work with this group: the value of understanding the "whole-istic" nature of the Five Element/Twelve Function model and the necessity for me to do as little as possible to support the group.

Take a Whole-istic Approach

While each of the five energies makes its own distinct contribution, together the energies define the life force of a human system. Being able to appreciate the integrated nature of this energy system is an essential step and a useful point of clarification for the observer utilizing this model. Appreciating all energy manifestations in a group as valuable or important is key. Rather than being confounded by the multiple and various energy findings, I found it helpful to consider each finding as a part of a mosaic—the beauty of which is best appreciated when viewed in its completeness. In this particular intervention, I got a second opportunity to see each energy and the relationship between the energies. I was prepared to be open to and alert for signs of all the energies, appreciating the impact of each on the others.

Maintaining a whole-istic view during the consultation reinforced another primary aspect of the model: understanding the connection between the observer and the group. This precept has a direct bearing on success. This required that I see and be in the group's energy while actively managing my own state of balance. During the session, I was struck by manifestation of my own Water energy. Water can be forceful or it can take on the dimensions of its container. I determined that remaining "fluid" with this group was the more appropriate intervention rather than forcing them into my predetermined agenda. I was conscious of the need to actively assess the group's status and needs, using findings to drive my interventions. If I had intervened from a state of personal imbalance or to suit my own energy preferences, the results would have been short term and produced potentially ineffective actions.

Follow the Law of Least Action

The second principle was the responsibility to start with the smallest action that would make a positive difference—known as the Law of Least Action. Rather than spending hours fully detailing the day's work or predetermining the outcomes of the session, I made the commitment to work within the group's energy and use its needs to guide my interventions. In respecting where the group was and suspending judgment, I was able to work around the edges of the group. Doing so decreased the potential to forcefully change the group. The Law of Least Action requires a coupling of patience with flexibility, trust, and careful consideration. By committing to the observer role throughout the entire process rather than just up to the point of diagnosis, I was open to listening as a receptive and active process rather than simply taking in and categorizing messages, words, and sounds. One way that the Five Element/Twelve Function model is effective is that it takes into account a plethora of information from sensations, movement, configuration, and emotions to help determine interventions.

Law of Least Action—

The Chinese believe in the natural ability of the body to regain balance or reestablish health. Therefore, interventions to regain balance or health should be kept to a minimum. For example in an acupuncture treatment, the fewer needles used by the practitioner to establish energy flow the better. Using this same thinking, a person practices the Law of Least Action by using fewer interventions, trusting the group to do what it needs to regain effectiveness.

In this intervention, I addressed the presence of the Water imbalance by giving things to the group (such as resources, a statement, and a process) rather than demanding more from the group. The latter would likely have reinforced or accentuated the already observed fear and rigidity (Water). By merely suggesting a change in the mode of communication— the Law of Least Action—I obtained valuable information that served as the foundation for substantial movement in this session and in the group's future.

Understanding and applying the Law of Least Action is one of the more difficult principles in this energy system. It requires a basic faith in the group's ability to shift in accordance with its own energy needs and in its own time. The rush to outcomes, a need for substantive change in short periods of time or significant control issues can interfere with the natural flow of energy. The observer's own agenda must be to use a light touch, to work on the periphery of the group.

Summary

Water...fluid, powerful, and the first of the five energies. It glistens, roars, cleanses, and is still, sometimes frozen. The purpose and resource work in the Water energy create the foundation for the next energy, Wood, with its motivating, action-oriented nature.

5

Wood—
A Vision and a Plan

Diane Miller

The wind appears and the trees gently shift in its
midst reaching and stretching skyward
with roots deeply anchored below.
The beginning blooms grace sturdy branches
supporting buds dipped in new green.
Marching bands circle in formation below.
Ah, a breath of spring in the air!

With spring's arrival, there is soil to till and plantings to buy. Planning to renew yard and home begins after a season of dormancy. The east holds the dawning sun, which reflects on trees with limbs bearing scattered buds of silvery green—the signs of an awakening from winter's rest. It is a season of growth. Doors open and neighbors renew their relationships. Is there anything more refreshing than the first hints of spring, the season of Wood energy?

Spring is a time of action. The office needs a fresh coat of paint, files need arranging, work needs organizing. Schedules are mapped out and visions are revisited. Teams emerge from a period of quiet reflection. Initiatives are begun with new excitement and decisions are made. This energy is upright and accelerating. It is arousal guided by practicality and pragmatism. Wood energy develops unique ways to meet these challenges in a determined, independent, and willful manner.

Wood supports the organization or individual with its thorough and inquisitive nature, clarifying the vision with foresight and keen judgment. It is the courage to take on the adventure, never bored with minute detail. "I can see a way through this," says this energy. It is driven by the need to stay in motion. Those who are Wood types forcefully and boldly direct a venture, knowing when to yield, flex, and adapt to the strong wind of resistance. It is a contest, after all. At times, Wood is self-serving and always confident.

Two good examples of Wood energy can be found in the political arena: Bob Dole and Hillary Rodham Clinton. Another well-known figure, Jane Fonda, models Wood's capacity for assertiveness, truthfulness, and willingness to take risks.[1] All three demonstrate a decisive, strategic leadership nature.

Wood types, with their capacity to be future-oriented, are known to clearly establish their own roles and roles for others in an organization, adding impetus to a change process or creating a foundation for a new department. A team's ability and efficiency is supported by a decisive, action-oriented leader who takes charge in an emergency, directing effort by shouting orders to the troops.

Wood energy puts plans and ideas into actions with newfound energy. It is purposeful, and driven by a righteous cause. It emerges as a methodical, continuous, internal force with a clear ebb and flow. It is a vital sap surging through the structure of a change process.[2] Wood energy is initial excitement, and is often coupled with the hesitancy to leave the comfort of the silent, still winter (Water).

It can also be too many rules with insistence on rigid adherence. Self-assurance can take the form of self-importance.[3] Its pioneering spirit runs the risk of shattering the status quo with a plan that is too ambitious. Its reactive nature or ready-fire-aim needs to be tempered to give others time to adjust and make the needed transition. Indeed, the commanding, assertive, and self-assured nature of Wood can be viewed as badgering and intimidating. It pushes the limits, seeking to be challenged and to challenge. It is a speed-driven, action orientation stated as, "Let's get on, with the getting on" that rattles the quietness of Water and the steadiness of Earth. In the quest to be first, there are times that Wood is perceived as working against others rather than with others. The Chinese philosopher Lao-Tzu urges a healthy balance of Wood with the use of words, "the hard and stiff will be broken...the supple will prevail."[4]

The emotion associated with Wood is anger. Though often defined as a negative, this emotion can be energizing, motivating, and constructive. It can be the impetus for defensive responses and competitive positioning. Anger can signal dissatisfaction with the current situation, fueling a team effort to outline steps for survival or recapturing its competitive edge. Wood creates a useful tunnel vision that increases focus and concentration. It also can create a strong social bond, uniting a "we" against an army of "they" who pose a threat. Wood has even been used by activist groups to raise attention to a social injustice, creating the nucleus for social reform.[5]

Yin and Yang of Wood

...On Sunday, I identify my goals for the work week. Monday morning I establish a plan for each goal; some are nonnegotiable. Other plans are flexible and can be easily altered as additional demands emerge. I find the structure reassuring. It supports my getting things done and guides how I spend my time. When I speak with clients I can give them a clear time for filling their requests. Working long hours is no chore as long as I control my pace and make decisions for myself. I always say: plan the work and work the plan...

The yin organ of Wood identified in the Five Element model is the liver, which is responsible for cleansing the system and making decisions about what is essential or needs to be eliminated. A healthy liver, referred to in eastern medicine as the Commander of the blood, provides strength and vitality to the system.[6] It creates an openness to new ideas and experiences. Effective communication with others and personal expressions of creativity are evidence of healthy Wood.

The yang organ of Wood is the gallbladder. This organ concentrates and stores bile used for the digestion of fat so it can be eliminated via the intestines. In eastern medicine, the gallbladder rules the body's kingdom, a careful decision maker with impeccable judgment who moderates any recklessness or impulsive behavior and supports the expression of emotion.[7] If the blood is left uncleansed by an unhealthy liver, the whole system becomes bloated and toxic. If the gallbladder fills with calcified stones, there is intense pain. If an individual or organization lacks sufficient Wood energy, drive evaporates and visions go unarticulated. The vital energy for change and survival is lost.

Wood Energy in Individuals and Teams

Wood energy types are driven by detail and are considered to use an elaborate approach to getting things done. Calendars and lists and lots of information are central to decision making and action planning—a place for everything and nifty little boxes that hold things, preferably marked so they can easily be found. These types are obsessed with finding solutions; change is their middle name. Not averse to long hours of focused concentration, it is suddenly 5:00 p.m. and the Wood individual asks, "Where has the time gone? Did I have lunch?" One also sees Wood energy in the flair for time management and organizing things.

Imbalances in Wood occur when plans are not created or a group is hopelessly locked in indecision, stopping the system and leaving members angry about experiencing another example of chronic startup. If implementation is not begun, despite evidence for needed change or actions are out of step with the data, effectiveness can be affected by a Wood imbalance.

Wood is represented by the color green. Its sensory organ is the eye. Wood is nourished by Water or is the child of Water. In normal states, Wood energy stays busy doing what is purposeful. It is a discerning eye that distinguishes important from artifact, and information from data. Shouts or staccato voice quality best exemplify the sounds of Wood energy. Wood is noted in the 11 p.m. to 3 a.m. time period. Food cravings for lemon, chicken, vinegar, crab apples, or broccoli demonstrate a need to refill Wood.

In the second stage of an organizational change process, Wood energy provides a critical function by helping a group to map out the plan. The scheduling and time-keeping tendencies of Wood are needed assets at this point. Strategies and organization must precede the communicating, networking, and problem solving of the Fire phase of the change. In the Wood stage, one can sense the emerging urgency. A number of questions can be asked to ensure success in this step: What can we do to make this a success? How much of this is negotiable? What parts are essential?

The plan needs to have clear borders and processes for the group to make decisions that align the plan with the vision. The team that attends to Wood will confidently move ahead, fully assured that this is the right thing to do. All of these support and mobilize a full team effort and collaboration in the Fire stage of the change, which, in turn, supports the productivity and distribution of the change in the Earth stage of the process.

Table 5-1 summarizes Wood energy. This energy provides the ability to plan, organize, adapt, decide, clarify, and structure.[8] When these functions are intact or balanced, the system or individual functions well. When any of these are deficient, it becomes inefficient. For example, a plan without decision making leads to a state often referred to as analysis paralysis. In addition, attempting to organize files without folders or a file drawer (structure) leads to a very messy work space, making it hard to see anything besides mounds of papers.

Table 5-1: Wood Energy Overview

Season	Spring
Color	Green
Voice Tone	Shout
Emotion	Anger
Organs	Liver & Gallbladder
Motivation	To Grow
Thought Process	Analytic
Personality Type	Commander

Signs of Imbalance

When Wood energy is out of balance, the individual may become arrogant and/or demonstrate unhealthy expressions or degrees of anger. The usual assertiveness of Wood energy is transformed into aggression. The drive to pursue challenge becomes reckless. Communication becomes more clipped as the anger rises. There are signs of antagonism. Tyrannical behaviors are cited by others (see Table 5-2).

Table 5-2: Wood Energy in Work Groups/Organizational Life

Characteristics Indicating Balance	Characteristics Indicating Imbalance
Confidence	Works to exhaustion
Direct/assertive	Defensiveness leading to conflict with others
Well-thought-out path to implementation	Excessive structure & hierarchical relationships
Committed, willing to fight for the outcome	Analysis paralysis
	Apathetic about moving forward or accepting responsibility
	Inflexible & rule-bound

In Table 5-2, column one represents behaviors that indicate a healthy balance of wood energy while column two represents unhealthy or imbalanced wood energy.

In organizations, groups design plans and actions that are confrontational rather than cooperative. These plans are often self-serving rather than serving others. There is undue adherence to actions and processes rather than attention to outcomes. Rules take on too great an importance even when they don't make sense. Structure is viewed as the cure for all ills. Teams become immovable, fighting with others to defend their turf. Wood energy imbalances lead to intolerance and impatience. There is too much discipline, even punishment for failures. It will take using nature's wisdom, specifically the K'o or Control cycle, to constrain or balance this imbalance.

When Wood is depleted individuals become ineffectual and unable to make a decision "if my life depended on it." And when there is action, it is erratic or fickle. Teams show ambivalence and do not see things through. They begin to feel powerless. They compromise on those things that are important. Analysis paralysis sets in even though the associated emotion is frustration. Despite the elaborate plans, no action is seen.

Indeed, individuals can become suspicious of others' actions and are sure that there is a "hidden agenda" in play. Blatant breaking of the rules occurs. The desire to act and do is soon replaced by apathy. There is second guessing and an unwillingness to accept the responsibility to move ahead. The paralysis can be displayed in seeking an expert to tell them what to do. The healthy Wood energy of feeling invincible is replaced by vulnerability and a loss of control. "There is nothing that I can do" is a signature statement of Wood imbalance. Actions taken can be disjointed or ill-timed, which others see as impulsive and erratic, or the failure to exercise good judgment.

Because Wood energy is the parent of, or feeds, Fire, an imbalance in Wood energy slows problem solving and leads to inactivity. Confidence, commitment, and assertiveness are lost as the imbalance of Wood energy leads to reckless and confrontational behavior. Difficulties with developing cooperative approaches emerge.[9] The change process stagnates. Nature's wisdom calls for The Law of Least Action, Control cycle and Creation cycle to address these unhealthy imbalances.

Case Study

I was engaged as a mentor in a relationship with an individual as she learned the ropes in her role as an educator. She was to develop new courses and teach several established programs. After an initial orientation of five days and with the assurance that ongoing support was available, Jean was sent out to begin presenting. Evaluations from participants attending these programs were reviewed and results were recorded in a spreadsheet format.

In early programs, the ratings had been at the "Very good" to "Excellent" range for both presenter and presentation. After the first four programs, ratings became more erratic, largely falling in the range from "Fair" to "Excellent." I discussed my concerns with Jean, asking for her thoughts on these findings. She stated that the groups had all been tough and she identified a variety of environmental factors she felt had an impact on the group and the program. I asked for her action plan to raise scores and she committed to writing her personal assessment of each program and the comments on evaluations she received, and also said she would provide her development plan for areas of improvement.

However, instead of the expected improvements, Jean's scores fell to the "Poor" to "Average" range. She submitted the evaluations without the agreed-on assessment and development plan. Though repeatedly requested, none were forthcoming. I met again with Jean to discuss program evaluations and she stated that I was being too critical and that she was angry I had requested the meeting. I reiterated the goal of routinely achieving

"Good" to "Excellent" scores and we agreed to team-teach the next program. Jean expressed confidence that by observing me teach specific sections that she felt weaker in, she would be able to improve. She identified specific sections that she was confident in teaching and began her preparation for the session.

Yet, during the team teaching, Jean repeatedly left the room rather than closely observing sections I taught. During her teaching time, major content areas of each section were under-taught, and she omitted entire aspects or critical points within these sections. When I asked Jean for her self-assessment of her teaching, she mentioned feeling very distracted by other things. Evaluations for her teaching again ranged from "Poor" to "Average." Comments shared by participants were discounted by Jean as finger pointing. She stated, "I think I teach these sections just fine." She abruptly terminated the meeting earlier than the scheduled ending time.

Energy Assessment

How do we set people up to be successful? Four helpful interventions are: providing orientation (Water), structure (Wood), forming a relationship with the individual (Fire), and giving ongoing support through a mentoring relationship (Earth). Creating situations for additional problem solving (Fire), action planning (Earth), and a review of evaluations to assist in meeting desired outcomes (Metal) are critical. When these are coupled with a team-teaching approach (Earth), all five energies are called into play.

My assessment of Jean indicated an imbalance in Wood energy through the following manifestations:

- Quick start-up and short-term results
- Failure to "see" that her decisions related to her teaching approaches negatively impacted others
- Failure to map a course for change
- Planning without follow-through
- Anger
- Need for independence rather than adherence to expectations
- Apathy
- Collapsed effort; failure to implement positive, corrective action steps
- Indifference to established structure
- Judgment and criticism of participants and her mentor

Pitfalls and Processes for Balancing Wood

Unhealthy Wood energy is one of the more difficult of the imbalances to address. When confronted with an individual like Jean, who repeatedly fails to accept standard support and work a plan, it is tempting to take the responsibility on yourself or delegate it to someone who will get it done. Yet, these actions do little to correct the Wood deficiency. When faced with Wood imbalances, you have three choices:

1. Work within the energy, making the yin-yang connection.
2. Feed the energy, using the parent of the energy that is distorted (the Cycle of Creation).

3. Restrain the energy by using the Control cycle.

In my initial interventions with Jean, I attempted to balance the connection between yin and yang. These interventions included:

- Creating achievable expectations (planning and clarifying)
- Assisting Jean in understanding how to be an effective presenter (strategizing)
- Providing Jean with the decision about what she wanted to teach during the team-teaching session (promoting independence)
- Visually capturing feedback from participants
- Soliciting her thoughts on how to resolve issues (decision making)
- Suggesting remedies, offering her autonomy in selecting those she deemed as most useful (adapting)
- Overlooking her demonstrations of anger, not responding in a like confrontational communication pattern

Secondly, I employed the following Creation cycle interventions in Water energy:

- Restating our purpose, to offer a quality program to all participants
- Providing subsequent direction
- Restating target ratings as "Good" to "Excellent" (setting limits)
- Requesting development plans (defining boundaries)

Finally, I used Control to balance Wood through the use of Metal energy interventions:

- Providing evaluation data over time with emphasis on patterns (evaluating)
- Tracking all ratings for programs and Jean's scores as a presenter (comparing)
- Offering Jean, after providing a system of support, the choice to improve and continue or else stop teaching the program (improving or eliminating)

However, Jean's energy did not change with the first two cycles of intervention. She withdrew further from subsequent contacts, eventually becoming apathetic about her performance with this and other programs. She left the department shortly after being presented the choice to improve or stop teaching the program.

Staying in the process when immediate results are not obtained can be difficult. Nonetheless, the Law of Least Action guides us to use the yin-yang connection first, before the use of the Cycle of Creation and, finally, the Control cycle. Staying even tempered and not responding in kind to anger is essential in managing our own energy. Anything less potentiates an undue influence by the facilitator in the change process as well as possibly damaging what could and is supposed to be a therapeutic relationship between the mentor and mentee.

Summary

Wood provides an organization with an energy that is robust and can be a catalyst for growth. Wood energy is tenacious, direct, and "tells it like it is." In the Chinese text, *The I Ching*, Wood is described as adapting itself to obstacles and bending around them. Wood energy is movement and action in an individual with a firm sense of self who had been idle or dormant. In an organization, it is evident in plans that lead to decisions that further a change process.

Wood is spring, long awaited after a cold winter. New buds of plants and plans signal a change process to be welcomed. Nature's Wisdom is evident everywhere. Green and fresh and spring—it is reinvigorating!

6

Fire—
The Snap, Crackle
& Pop

Jo Manion

Brightly colored hot air balloons
filling the clear blue summer sky.
Rollicking laughter during good times with friends.
Bright, electric fireworks lighting up the night sky.
The warm closeness of loved ones.
Joy of work.
The happy exuberance of a puppy at play.
Giggles of a child being tickled.
Listening to the corn grow on a hot Midwest July day.

Fire energy is the height of yang in the cycle. This is energy at its most expansive and exuberant. The preparatory work of the previous energies, Water and Wood, has produced results and they are spectacular! Fire energy provides the animation and excitement in life. Unlike Water, it knows no boundaries. It is effusive and warming, dynamic and exciting. Unlike the elaborate structure of Wood energy as seen in plants and trees with their trunk, bark, leaves, and clearly defined root system, Fire energy cannot be contained by structure. It is expansive in the same sense as Wood energy as it reaches upward, but it surpasses the heights attained by Wood because it is not bound by rigid structure in quite the same way.

From the power of Fire we get the ability to create and sustain relationships with other people. We communicate with each other in a manner that is open and sharing, building on the trust engendered by healthy Water. We respect the boundaries and limitations of our relationships as defined by healthy Wood energy, yet we are free to explore and go beyond these arbitrarily set limits. Healthy relationships are dynamic, shifting, and always growing to new heights. We expand and stretch, constantly seeking new opportunities for sharing with each other. Fire energy is the spark, the tingle, and the passion found in our relationships with others. It animates our lives and produces a sense of synergy, the understanding that together we are much greater than each of us alone would be.

A recognition of and a respect for our interdependence are the primary dynamics of Fire energy. Fire is that part of us which accepts that we exist in relationship with others, that life is a web of interconnections so complex it is almost inconceivable to our minds. Thus, healthy Fire energy helps us recognize the need for cooperation and coordination of our efforts. It insists on our setting priorities because we face simply too many choices and possibilities. Instead, we must sort through and determine which actions, relationships, initiatives, and projects are the ones in which to invest our energy.

Fire energy is naturally seductive. Healthy, balanced Fire reaches out and draws others to it. The positive expression of Fire energy is contagious and attractive to others. It is seen in a newborn's response to his or her parents in the form of smiles and gurgles, creating a powerful bond that must be strong enough to hold through times when the child seems less lovable and convenient (for instance, at 3 a.m.). It is also present at a party, where a small group of people who are laughing and clearly enjoying themselves often begin to attract others. All of us naturally gravitate to Fire energy, including in workplaces where employees enjoy each other and their work, where fun and humor are part of every day.

The natural seductiveness of Fire energy can be easily seen in the home where a fire burns in the fireplace on a cold, crisp evening. A hot, brightly burning fire snaps, crackles, and shoots sparks upward and out. The vivid brightness of the flames fascinates us. People are drawn closer to the hearth, captivated by the sight and warmth of this expansive energy. We sit by the fire and take in its heat, mesmerized by the sight. Sitting too close to a roaring fire, however, is uncomfortable. And, in the same way that we move away from the heat that is too intense, so do we move away from the individual exhibiting too-intense Fire energy. The fire analogy helps us also understand the difference between yin and yang Fire energy. A roaring fire, as just described, is a more Yang aspect with its voracious energy while the steady, glowing coals after the fire has burned down is more typical of yin Fire energy.

* * *

Summer is the season of Fire energy (see Table 6-1). The sun beats down hot on the earth and you can see the waves of heat shimmer and rise from the pavement. The coolness of spring and the fresh growth, as buds burst into flower and summer crops pierce through the earth's covering, give way to the expansive growth of the warmth of summer. The rapid expansion is clear evidence of Fire energy. Summer has traditionally been a time of less work and more play. In American culture especially, summer heralds vacations from school, trips with the family, and going away to camp, all of which represent times of enjoyment and planned leisure. We have worked hard during the winter and spring, laying the foundation, and now it is time to enjoy this growth period.

Table 6-1: Fire Energy Overview

Season	Summer
Color	Red
Voice Tone	Laughter
Emotion	Joy
Organs	Small intestine/Heart
	Pericardium/Triple heater
Motivation	To integrate
Thought Process	Associative
Personality Type	Communicator

Red is the color associated with Fire energy. Individuals with Fire energy often have a rosy, even a ruddy, complexion and usually blush quite easily. The area around the eyes and temple often takes on a reddish hue as well. People with strong Fire energy often wear red and are attracted to the color. "A strong, bright red skin color indicates an excess of Fire, while an ashen, pale complexion points to a deficiency."[1]

Joy is the emotion associated with Fire energy. The most common description of joy in our language relates to the expansive quality that is characteristic of this emotion. It has been described as a state of heightened energy, exhilaration, and elation. "The emotions of elation fill us and lift us up."[2]

Interestingly, scholars who study emotions have concluded that the purpose and function of joy is simply its expression. Izard notes that joy operates as a universal signal of readiness for friendly interaction. Kast says that joy is "the foundation of alliance and solidarity...Elated emotional states make us feel connected to other persons, to our inner world, perhaps even to the cosmos."[3]

Joy strengthens social bonds. Izard notes that the first "sure sign of joy in the human infant is the social smile."[4] Furthermore, "by the principles of contagion, empathy, and facial feedback, joy expression can contribute to the well-being of the social surround (milieu)."[5] If we understand that a primary role of Fire energy revolves around people and relationships, it is no surprise that scholars find the primary motivation of joy is in its fostering of social connections and relationships.

Joy is a natural outgrowth of expansive Fire energy. "In ecstatic joy we may feel light and bouncy, or that we could soar, or that we are soaring and that everything has a different perspective because of our unusual vantage point."[6] "Every movement connected with joy, even a quiet joy, is an elevating movement, relieving us of our normal weightiness, causing us to rise up and see matters from another perspective."[7] Kast created a beautiful passage in her book that describes joy and healthy Fire energy:

> *A lantern is lit, syllables shimmer, everything floats upward. These are symbols for expressions of joy. You may be aware that when you laugh, the corners of your mouth normally curve upward; your face floats a little. Your eyes start to glow. Flickering and glowing are facial expressions. You leap for joy, or at least you would like to. The effect of joy is to counteract the pull of gravity and thus represents the force of levity. No wonder we always hear that joy is playful. With joy we overcome resistance and so naturally find a way to transcend ourselves.[8]*

Laughter is the sound associated with Fire energy. The voice is warm, more rapid, and the tone and pitch are higher. Researchers Pittam and Scherer note that joy was one of the few positive emotions studied in terms of vocalization. In most instances, it was studied in the form of elation rather than more subdued expressions such as enjoyment or happiness. They discovered changes in frequency and vocal tone, an increase in high-frequency energy, and an increase in rate of articulation.[9]

Fire is the only energy that is connected with four rather than two organ networks. The yang organs are the small intestine and the Triple Heater. The yin organs are the heart and

Heart Protector, or pericardium. Metaphorically these organs are responsible for the "outreach, connection, and exuberant energy that characterize the Fire element."[10] These organs also have clear physical functions in the body. The heart circulates the vital life-giving blood throughout the system. It controls the pulses that provide an indication of the quality of the circulatory system. The small intestine receives partially digested food from the stomach and its job is to filter and separate the pure from the impure. The impure products are then released into the large intestine for elimination from the system. The third organ related to Fire energy is the pericardium, the lining that covers the heart. It is thought to protect the heart, both literally and metaphorically. The Chinese believe the Heart Protector provides a buffer for the heart from over-stimulation and emotional shock. The final organ network associated with Fire energy is the only one in Chinese medicine that does not have a corresponding physical organ structure identified in Western medicine.

Once you understand the function of the Triple Heater in Chinese medicine, it becomes clear that such a function also exists in our physical bodies. The Triple Heater is the coordination and regulation system that controls and coordinates the function of all other organs. Perhaps it is more closely akin to our endocrine or nervous system with their fine sense of attunement and interdependence. At least metaphorically, the Triple Heater is responsible for the relationships between all other organ systems and the body.

Fire Energy in the Individual

Fire energy people are known as great communicators (see Table 6-1). They thrive on talking and connecting with others, whether in their family life, at work or with friends. These people come home from a good party and are so wound up they cannot sleep, their heart is racing. Their enthusiasm for others continues long beyond the actual contact.

People with healthy Fire energy are usually articulate and persuasive. In the professional speaking arena, these are the great motivational speakers. They exude energy and excitement, and their posture is usually quite expansive. They are characterized by many freely flowing and exuberant hand and arm gestures—and a resistance to remaining behind a fixed podium.

Joy, the emotion of Fire energy, is highly desirable in our work and in our personal environments and relationships. It is expressed in laughter and gaiety in its most outward form and in pleasure and warm feelings in its quieter manifestation. It is sought when absent and highly valued when present. The individual with strong Fire energy is often referred to as "high energy" and draws others to him or her.

In the public arena, Robin Williams is a good example of Fire energy. He is a remarkable comedian with the ability to spontaneously help us see the humor in all things. Generating laughter in others is his goal and when he is on a "roll" he is almost manic. Goldie Hawn is another well-known figure who comes to mind when thinking of Fire energy. She is vivacious, and has an infectious laugh and a smile that has often been described as one that "lights up the room when she walks in." You want to laugh with her.

Fire Energy in the Organization

An organization with healthy Fire energy is in an expansive mode; it is at the peak of its performance. For optimum Fire energy, the organization has fully completed the work of the Water and Wood phases. Priorities are set according to the degree to which they fit the mission and purpose of the organization. People know what the priorities are and they know that although daily crises might intervene, it is not acceptable to lose sight of the essential priorities. Cooperation and coordination between people, teams, shifts, departments, and services exist at a high level. People are informed of progress and information is shared openly. Thus, employees and managers know what is happening in other parts of the organization in addition to their own areas of responsibility.

Effective, mature teams are a reality in this organization. Teams are more than lip service. People work well with each other and accept mutual accountability for the outcomes of the organization. When things go wrong, there is little finger-pointing and blaming; instead, people work together to figure out how to correct the situation. Problem-solving skills are used to actually resolve problems and make forward progress on the issues faced. Communication between people is primarily positive.

The working environment is a high-energy, positive place where people experience and express joy. Excitement and enthusiasm for working together and for the possibilities that the future holds is evident. Working relationships are healthy and help solidify employee commitment to the organization. There is warm regard and respect for each other.

Signs of Imbalance

The individual with excess Fire energy is hyper-excitable and easily distracted, finding it difficult to remain focused on any one task or thing. Anxiety with heart palpitations and a rapid pulse are often symptoms of excessive Fire energy. The person's behavior can almost be described as manic, an out-of-control excitement or state of over-stimulation. Laughter and giggling is inappropriate or excessive and may be annoying to others. Often described as "having too many irons in the fire" or "burning the candle at both ends," this individual easily becomes depleted of energy. Deficient Fire energy manifests differently. The person appears almost without affect of any kind, seeming dull and unresponsive, lethargic and apathetic. There simply is no light in the person's eyes.

Deficient energy—

an imbalance in energy that results in a loss of health or effectiveness.

In the organization Fire energy imbalances have similar manifestations. A frenetic pace and a sense of underlying anxiety are common, evidenced by the sense that, "We won't be successful if we don't..." This anxiety often plays out in the large number of high-priority projects that are "absolutely essential for our success and future viability." In addition, the crisis orientation of the culture precludes people from focusing on projects and change initiatives long enough to accomplish any results. "All we do is put out fires" is a common refrain. In one organization, the CEO handed out a fireman's red helmet to each of the managers to make note and light of the crisis orientation of the culture. Employees and managers alike are often interrupted and unable to complete tasks and responsibilities because of the distractions in the system. Not only is there an excessive number of largely unproductive meetings, they may actually be scheduled simultaneously.

Work relationships are also affected when Fire energy is out of balance. Cooperation is not freely offered; instead, departments and services compete with each other in unproductive ways. Departments and leaders vie for attention and recognition, often at the expense of others. Communication suffers as information is withheld, blocked or inappropriately delivered. For example, one group of workers with deficient Fire energy decided that face-to-face communication and forging relationships was just too taxing; they had reached the point where their relationships with each other occurred only through the electronic mail system.

When Fire is out of balance, the organization can lose its ability to discern what is really important and its effectiveness in establishing appropriate priorities is hampered. Priorities may be identified, but the instant something that seems more important comes along, the previous project or task is dropped. In other words, the urgencies of today must be dealt with immediately and as a result organizations lose sight of priorities previously established. When those priorities are development projects or initiatives undertaken to strengthen the system for the future (some of those yin, "soft side" of management functions), this has the effect of reprioritizing them to a lesser level without a discussion even taking place.

Out-of-balance Fire energy also results in lack of coordination and cooperation between people, teams, departments, services, and organizations. The right hand does not know what the left hand is doing. Key stakeholders are left out of initiatives and only discover later that an important project was undertaken. Problem solving is given only lip service—people tend to process the same problems over and over again, never actually solving them. This may happen because of a lack of skills or an organizational culture that lacks support for effective problem solving. Many people note the irony in the statement: "We never have time to do it right, but we always seem to have time to do it over."

Another sign of imbalance in Fire energy in organizations manifests itself in a lack of interpersonal skills and unhealthy working relationships. Getting things accomplished occurs on a barter system, for instance, "You do this for me and I will help you out later." This creates a culture of unhealthy competitiveness and using each other. Those who are ambitious often succeed at the expense of colleagues and coworkers. Groups of people may coexist, but true teams are a rarity. It is a world where it is "every man for himself (or woman for herself)." The mutual accountability that marks a true team simply does not exist (see Table 6-2).

Table 6-2: Fire Energy in Work Groups/Organizational Life

Characteristics Indicating Balance	Characteristics Indicating Imbalance
Clear priorities	Communication problems
High level of cooperation	No clear priorities or everything is critical
Healthy working relationships	Frenetic pace, people feel fragmented
Effective teams	Crisis mentality
Open, positive communication	Relationship problems

In Table 6-2, column one represents behaviors that indicate a healthy balance of Fire energy while column two represents unhealthy or imbalanced Fire energy.

Fire Energy in Review

Fire energy is the culmination of the work of Water and Wood energies. It is a peak experience, the most expansive energy within the Five Element/Twelve Function model. It is a joyous time because we see things coming together, results being produced, people working well together, teams gelling and experiencing a great deal of enjoyment in life and work. But Fire energy is seductive and can burn too brightly. Rising too quickly, expending our energy without regard to replenishment leads to depletion of this vital force.

Case Study

An organization that exemplifies Fire energy is a community-based, not-for-profit health care system. When I was there, it was engaged in fundamentally changing its structure and the way it delivered patient care. I was invited to the organization after several managers and key organizational leaders heard my presentation on team-based organizations. I met with the executive team to determine whether my services would be useful as they progressed through a major work reengineering and redesign project. My contract with the organization ended up spanning a three-year period.

My primary services included establishing teams, educating employees, and preparing managers for the cultural transformation to an empowering form of leadership. Every department and service was actively involved in restructuring itself and redesigning its work to increase quality and efficiency of performance. The organization had also embarked on a massive expansion project involving the acquisition of a home health agency, a long-term care facility, the implementation of a new comprehensive cardiac program, construction of a new wing on the hospital, the development of an insurance product, and the merger with other organizations in its geographical area.

Mark, the CEO, was a dynamic and charismatic leader. Articulate and persuasive, he became quite passionate about the organization and its goals whenever he met with groups of colleagues, employees or physicians. While listening to him, employees and leaders alike found it difficult to resist whatever he suggested. A great communicator, Mark would hold "Town

Hall" meetings and talk at length about the vision for the organization and how they were going to work to attain this dream. Most people left feeling enthusiastic and positive. With a belief in the unlimited possibilities facing them, Mark had led this organization through many years of growth and expansion. However, his tendency to "overdrive" reached its peak during the final summer I worked with them. People in the organization were overwhelmed with the number of projects and initiatives they had undertaken. Employees, supervisors, managers, and executives were feeling as if they could not possibly keep up.

Mark asked me to facilitate a session with the executives and other key leaders in the organization to list and order their current projects and initiatives. I realized that the organization had been in "overdrive" for some time and was on a course to significant energy depletion if no intervention occurred. My role in the organization's initiatives, however, was in a more limited scope and precluded me from having a broader consultative and advisory role. Mark's invitation to me to facilitate this session was unexpected and came at an opportune time. It was the middle of summer and things had just gotten out of control there. Even Mark was having trouble "juggling all the balls." Previously successful executives and managers were finding themselves failing because of the fragmentation of their daily work life.

Prior to the session I brushed up on the Five Element/ Twelve Function model. I based my assessment of this organization's problem on my close working relationship with people in the organization over an extended period of time. I believed that the problem was excess Fire energy. These were the key observations leading to this conclusion:

- A demonstrated inability to distinguish between priorities—everything undertaken became a "front burner" project
- The vast number of major, complex projects that were undertaken simultaneously
- People feeling fragmented and distracted
- The executive group never became a team (this group completed all the preliminary structural work to become a team—identified values, a mission statement, working agreements, role definition, etc., when the COO arbitrarily decided that they did not need to work as a team although employees in the organization were expected to do so)
- Lack of cooperation between people and groups in the organization grew over the years as each was trying to protect its own project to ensure its completion
- Predominant language in the organization related to people feeling "burned out," busy "putting out fires," and having to "burn the candle at both ends"
- Several high achievers in the organization obviously depleted of essential energy, exhibiting little or no facial effect and an apathetic demeanor
- Deterioration of previously healthy relationships
- Key executive hospitalized repeatedly in the previous several months for cardiac problems
- Several other members of this leadership team recently diagnosed with hypertension

Need for Self-Assessment

I knew facilitating this group session would be difficult for me because one of my primary energies is Fire. I love the excitement, passion, and promise of this energy and this organization was exhibiting the same challenges in prioritizing that I have in my own work life. I knew I would need to be very careful to not fan the Fire energy or become seduced by the excitement of these many worthwhile projects the group was working to prioritize. Additionally I realized it would be important to manage my own energy during this half-day session. Therefore I chose to wear navy blue and avoid caffeine in any form prior to the session. I made a decision to take a lower-key approach and consciously control my own tendency to exude Fire energy. Additionally, I planned to remove myself from the group during break and go outside to sit next to a stream that split the property where the session was being held.

Intervention

I believed the best approach to this situation called for the use of the Control cycle to reduce some of the Fire energy. This could be accomplished by using Water to focus on the direct link between the project and the organization's mission and identifying the available resources for carrying out these initiatives.

The group began by listing all of the projects and initiatives that were underway. As items were added to the list, you could see the energy in the room change. Even individuals who were normally enthusiastic and positive began looking overwhelmed. This activity produced a formidable list of 108 items. It was no wonder people were fragmented and losing focus.

Once the list was established, the next step was to sort these initiatives by priority. The Fire energy in the room immediately began picking up again as evidenced by the passion with which people supported their pet project or special initiative. When it was suggested that a particular project was less than an "A" priority, the champion or sponsor of the project would articulately and persuasively identify the many reasons this project was critical. Seeing we were making no progress, I called a break. I suggested to people that they get outside and walk around a bit.

My plans to sit next to the quiet stream were thwarted when I was joined by several other members of the group. As the chatter and laughter flowed over me, I realized that this social interchange, although delightful, was simply feeding my Fire energy. I waited several minutes and then excused myself, heading to the women's restroom. Although not as aesthetically pleasing, I stood quietly in a closed stall for a few minutes. I took several deep breaths and just allowed myself to calm. Soon I felt centered and refocused on the process.

When we returned after break I sat in a chair (to express more Water energy while previously I had been standing) and asked people to look at the list and help me categorize the 108 items. This resulted in eight to ten categories such as: the construction project, automated documentation system, a new information system, reengineering and work redesign project, merger attempts, the insurance product, the new cardiac service, and so on. It became clear that the group also had some smaller, more isolated projects that did not directly relate to one of the major initiatives underway. These soon moved to the "B" list and some even to the "C" list.

I divided the group into four smaller groups and each of these groups took one to two of the major categories. I asked them to work together and discuss two issues:

- What are the resources required to carry out these initiatives effectively?
- How directly does this initiative relate to the primary purpose of the organization?

When the groups reconvened, the sorting process became easier. Several projects were deemed to be of more long-term impact and the group agreed that intense forward progress was a potentially destructive allocation of resources. The merger and acquisition of other facilities fell into this category. For several of the projects, a significant influx of resources would be needed initially for them to be successful, but these needs would taper off within three to four years. Reengineering and work redesign fit into this category as did the new cardiac services.

We soon realized that the organization did not have enough resources to adequately carry out the 108 projects. This was quite an eye-opener to the group, because they were unaware that the organization, which was financially well-situated, had failed to consider such resources as leadership skills and people's time. The group also discussed the sequencing of projects and determined that several of the major projects, such as implementation of the new cardiac services, would proceed faster and more effectively if employees within that service line were organized into work teams and participating at a high level of functioning.

In some instances the organization could purchase needed resources. For instance, contracting for implementation services for the new information system reduced the workload for current managers. A temporary construction supervisor was hired. Additional temporary external support for the reengineering effort also reduced the demands on internal managers. However, simply purchasing support was not enough. The group decided it needed to delay the implementation of the new cardiac services by a year and the merger activity indefinitely. This group of leaders left with a greater appreciation for the finite nature of people's energy and a commitment to being more realistic in the future.

Summary

The energy of connections and relationships, warmth and pleasure, Fire energy represents the social aspects of our world. An expansive energy form, it manifests in a range of expressions. Fire energy, joyful and radiant, is an essential part of any healthy system. It is contagious and spreads to others in a positive way. It is uplifting and takes us to the heights. Fire energy involves those peak experiences in life, when the work of Water and Wood energy burst forth into bright flame. "Fire is the power of radiant passion."[11]

Yet, excessive and unhealthy Fire energy can be just as devastating as any of the other energies. It can rage out of control, much like a forest fire, fed by enormous amounts of wood, destroying everything in its path. In individuals there is nothing subtle about out-of-control Fire energy as it manifests in manic or addictive behavior that has the tendency to drive others away. Lack of fire leads to a bleak and dark existence, one devoid of warmth and light. Healthy Fire energy brings joy, passion, light, and warmth into our lives.

7

Earth—
The Transition from
Yang to Yin

Sharon Cox

The fond memory of being snuggled in my Granny's bosom as she rocked me to sleep with an Irish lullaby...the wisdom in her wonderful stories and her calming way of letting me know "we can work this out." Feeling safe in my childhood with her unconditional love was my first experience of the nurturing aspects of Earth energy. I came to appreciate the ways she taught me self-reliance and a deep concern for the needs of others. Being with her was always like coming home and feeling centered in a deeply meaningful way.

With her unflappable nature, her love for "all God's children," and her quiet humility I came to know in a lasting way the essence of Earth energy.

In the late summer, harvest festivals celebrate the essence of Earth energy with their display of earth's abundance. Ripe fruits and grains are gathered, sorted, and stored to sustain the family through the upcoming winter. Nature is making the transition from yang to yin, from a time of growth and ripening to a time of pulling in and hibernating. This season of Earth energy is often referred to as Indian summer—a time when we can still feel the vibrancy of summer and yet also notice a smell of fall in the air. It is a transition time as we look back on what was, begin to process it, and prepare for closure and ending.

Table 7-1: Earth Energy Overview

Season	Late summer
Color	Yellow
Voice Tone	Singing or melodious
Emotion	Empathy
Organs	Stomach & spleen
Motivation	To stabilize
Thought Process	Cyclic
Personality Type	Peacemaker

Earth energy people are seen as peacemakers (see table 7-1). They thrive on maintaining harmony in the family and making everyone feel included. They love covered-dish dinners and they write thank-you notes reflecting how each contribution was special and appreciated. They are consummate arrangers, accepting of diversity, and able to find the common ground among even the most contentious. They often love to garden and feel the earth between their fingers. They are loyal, keep in touch with old friends, and often are seen as good mediators, unflappable and grounded. Where Fire energy attracts through charisma, Earth appeals to them with a sense of acceptance and nurturing—allowing them to feel centered. Those with an affinity for Earth energy find just as much pleasure in giving as receiving, and they value gifts that are hand-made rather than store bought.

Many are active in their community and concerned about giving back, not just taking. They are seen as being centered within and connected without, like the Earth Mother with that earthy aura rooted deep in the essence of sensuality... at one with their environment. Oprah Winfrey is a well-known personality with this primary energy and she often ends her talk show with tips on staying centered. Another well-liked TV personality with strong Earth energy was Charles Kuralt. A first-rate story teller, Kuralt had a knack for finding the good in people and making us all feel better about ourselves as we listened to his tales of interesting people he discovered in his travels throughout the country.

Both of these television personalities are well known for their ability to empathize with others and recognize the innate goodness in people. The Chinese associate this empathy as the emotion that predominates in the Earth element (see Table 7-1). Another characteristic feature of Earth energy is the need for routine—finding comfort and stability in seasonal or daily routines. This appreciation for the cyclic nature of life is reflected in the organs the Chinese associate with Earth energy. They associate the stomach and spleen with Earth energy in that the stomach stores food, breaking it down into essential nutrients, which are transported to the spleen where they are transformed into energy (chi) and blood.[1] Regular, cyclical input of nutrients is required or the stomach fails to function properly and the body doesn't have the nutrients it needs, resulting in low energy. The Chinese see the spleen as transforming nutrients into energy and dispersing this throughout the body, mind, and spirit.[2] When this organ is dysfunctional there is typically a disturbance in digestion, lack of clarity or the inability to concentrate.[3]

Earth element is considered the transitional element between the forceful, active side (yang as found in the Wood and Fire energy) of the Five Element model and the quieter more reflective (yin) energy associated with Metal and Water (see Figure 7-1). For this reason the Chinese associate this midway element with the color yellow, which is in the middle of the color spectrum. Making the transition from the busy and productive side of the cycle to the replenishing side of the cycle is essential for an individual to sustain energy over time and have the necessary stamina to meet the demands of life. Much like a well-stocked pantry (representing the collection of the fruits of one's labor), Earth energy can meet the needs for nourishment and sustenance over the fall and winter months until the next growing season. These are the functions of the Earth element.

The sound or voice tone associated with Earth energy fits an empathetic personality with a singing or melodious quality, much like a radio announcer on an easy listening station. One of the key issues for those with an affinity for Earth energy, given their peacemaker nature, is how to manage their concern for others and still maintain boundaries. A failure to attend to this issue often leads to the imbalance in Earth energy as described below.

Figure 7-1: Expenditure—Replenishment Cycle

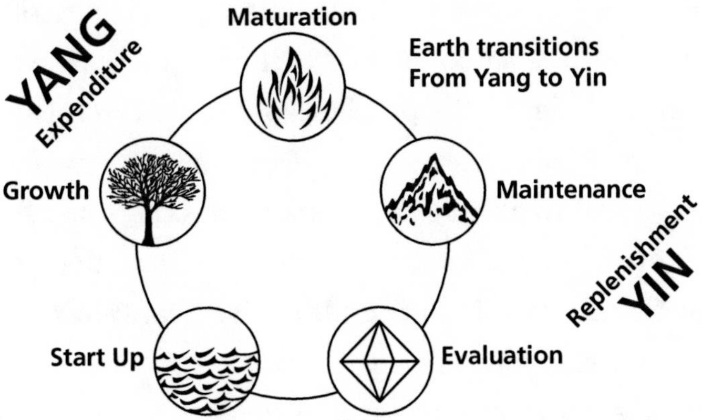

Signs of Imbalance

While Earth energy is the essence of caring and support, excess Earth energy is reflected in meddling behaviors, much like a busybody who has a lack of boundaries and a compulsion to solve the problems of others. These meddlesome, chronic worriers feel compelled to be all things to all people and are enmeshed in the lives of those around them, often perpetuating a soap opera-like existence. Those with excessive earth energy have the "disease to please," as Oprah has called it, and find it hard to believe that they are ever good enough. As a result they are often over-committed, find it very difficult to say no, and forget to take care of themselves. This codependent, fixer personality is all too common in the helping professions.

When Earth energy is deficient, an obvious neediness with deep feelings of inadequacy is apparent. The body lacks what it needs to sustain itself and illness is often evident, particularly digestive problems or eating disorders. A lack of energy and a sense of feeling "stuck" or unable to get on with projects or the chores of life are evident. The sense of inadequacy is usually accompanied by feelings of emptiness and fear of abandonment.[4] Feeling lethargic, worried, and weighed down by the problems of life are typical symptoms of deficient Earth energy. Individuals deficient in Earth energy often have clinging relationships with others and an addictive relationship with food. The sense that one does not deserve time for self-care and the guilt that self-care engenders are also characteristics of deficient Earth energy. Sluggishness and a general sense of heaviness often are reflected in strong attention to routine, methodically plodding through each day, and difficulty dealing with change or transitions.[5] Those with deficient Earth energy may have a "victim mentality" and see themselves as helpless in dealing with the difficulties of life.

Stuck energy—

Inability of an individual or group to move ahead due to an energy deficiency. For example, a person unable to grieve a loss (Metal) and regain a desire to live (Water) or a group that lacks trust in each other (Water) is unable to agree on a course of action (Wood).

Earth Energy in Groups and Organizations

On an individual level, Earth energy that is in balance is said to be stabilizing and supportive. The same is true in workgroups and organizations. When Earth energy is balanced in organizations, employees feel cared for as people and they know they are not just names on the schedule. There is a sense of commitment and loyalty to the organization as reflected in low turnover rates.

Employees feel supported in the sense that they have what they need to get their job done. Obviously this may be in the form of adequate and accessible supplies and equipment, but it also means availability of skills training and personal development opportunities. Employees are productive, not just busy, and can demonstrate clear outcomes that they work to improve over time. They are able to pace themselves as they deal with needed changes and are willing to do things differently to improve outcomes or service. They are not stuck in the mindset of "We have always done it this way," but instead can adapt to change and adjust their routines when needed. They have systems and procedures in place to ensure consistency of performance regardless of who is involved in carrying out a process (see Table 7-2).

Table 7-2: Earth Energy in Work Group/Organizational Life

Characteristics Indicating Balance	Characteristics Indicating Imbalance
Projects have measurable outcome & functions	Poor productivity— people feel overworked
Systems to ensure smooth operations	Inefficient systems— redundancy
Knowledge and experience integrated	Poor work flow— feeling blocked
Good employee morale	Lack of supplies and equipment
Low turnover	Customer service problems
	High rate of illness, absenteeism
	Quality of work life is poor

In Table 7-2, column one represents behaviors that indicate a healthy balance of Earth energy, while column two represents unhealthy or imbalanced Earth energy.

One of the characteristic attributes of work groups with healthy Earth energy is attention to balancing work and home life. Leaving work to attend a child's school play or soccer match is encouraged as is membership in health clubs or department athletic programs such as softball or volleyball leagues. With the increased emphasis on recruitment and retention of highly qualified employees, many organizations are now providing "concierge services," including dry cleaning, lawn service, carry-out dinners, and even gift-wrapping services. These convey the organization's support for employees and a desire to make their "life outside of work" a bit easier. This attention to supporting the staff and having them feel valued is at the heart of the philosophy espoused by many leading organizational consultants these days. Take care of the needs of your staff and they will take better care of patients. When patient satisfaction improves, market share increases, lawsuits decrease, and the bottom line improves.[6]

When Earth energy is out of balance in organizations and work groups, however, productivity and service delivery diminish (see Table 7-2). When Earth energy is seriously deficient, employees lack even the basic supplies and equipment they need and productivity suffers. Systems and processes are not established and so getting something done often depends on the force of personalities involved. In other words, the individual who knows how to bypass the formal system and knows who to call informally with a request is often most successful. When Earth energy is out of balance, employees feel scattered and overworked. Spending their time searching for needed equipment and supplies, they are working around inefficiencies in other departments. Often the rate of illness and use of sick days exceeds the norm because employees are chronically overextended. Yet there is a reluctance to change or manage needed transitions. This often appears in the organization as a reluctance to update routines and processes. A high value is placed on maintaining the status quo.

In systems where Earth energy is imbalanced, micro-management is often the norm. The same old problems get recycled, sometimes for years. The emphasis is on getting tasks done according to policy rather than focusing on outcomes and allowing for creativity and innovation. The peacemaker style is the norm; no one wants to rock the boat. Resistance to change is pervasive and a high premium is placed on maintaining traditions. Those who challenge the status quo are seen as troublemakers, not team players, and are sometimes excluded from group activities. There is a pervasive sense of apathy that "nothing is ever really going to change around here" and employees are apt to view change as something they can out-wait.

Earth Energy in Review

The importance of Earth's healthy energy in the workplace cannot be stressed enough. As mentioned in earlier discussions of the Shen cycle, Fire energy feeds Earth. Problem solving and teamwork (Fire) lead to productivity and service delivery (Earth) as reflected in well-managed outcomes. These outcomes are the basis for quality improvement efforts (Metal) and the ability to move into a new cycle. As logical as this may sound, the attention to outcomes and quality (the yin part of the cycle) are often overlooked in organizations that are preoccupied with multiple priorities and theme of the month change. All too often this pattern goes undetected until there is an obvious problem with turnover or an excessive rate of illness, indicating that employees are worn out, exhausted, and feeling unsupported.

The attention to outcomes—through evaluation, measuring, monitoring, benchmarking—is of utmost importance in completing the cycle and balancing the yang and yin of organizational life. We routinely have to pause and ask the question: "Are we being productive or just busy?" Failing to incorporate the yin aspects of the cycle is inherently dissatisfying in that we never get to enjoy the fruits of our labor (Earth) and experience the closure and pleasure of work well done (Metal).

As Earth energy allows us to transition from busyness through an evaluative stage to being reflective, it also has the effect of balancing Water energy that is excessive. This was presented earlier in the K'o cycle. Earth's effect on water is patently obvious when we see community volunteers piling up sandbags to protect homes and businesses in danger of being flooded by a raging river. The Earth literally holds back the water by its ability to absorb and distribute. The same impact is evident in organizations when we employ productivity measures (Earth) to monitor the use of personnel resources (Water) rather than giving the resources to those who make the most and loudest noise. Factoring in clinical outcomes and patient satisfaction data when starting a new service rather than just implementing a new service because it is the current fad reflects the use of Earth energy (outcomes) to balance Water (mission) (see Figure 7-2).

Figure 7-2: "Earth Holds Back Water"—K'o Cycle

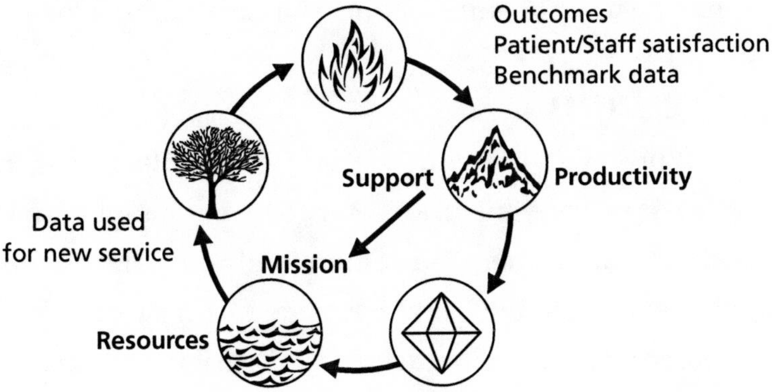

The third way we can work with Earth energy effectively is to ensure that the yin and yang aspects of Earth energy come together (juncture) to function well. An example of attending to this aspect of Earth energy is evident when organizations invest time, money, and effort in training employees for process improvement, tracking outcomes, and benchmarking with other facilities for best practices. When employees are given the tools they need (support), they can be more effective removing redundancy or streamlining processes, thereby increasing productivity (see Figure 7-2).

Whether we think of Earth energy in terms of support, productivity, or stability, it is easy to see why the Chinese refer to the central importance of this element. It is the source of our sense of equilibrium. When we feel out of balance or lose our sense of balance, for whatever reason, we intuitively long for a way to get centered and regain our sense of stability.

In organizational life, a sense of stability is reflected in smoothly running systems and processes, measurable outcomes, and employees who feel supported and valued as key players in the overall success of the organization. A review of the essential features of Earth energy in organizations (review Table 7-1) may be useful before reading the case study below.

Case Study

While working with a group of middle managers in a large tertiary care medical center on a nine-month project involving management education and staff development, I found myself meeting with a frustrated director of Materials Management (formerly known as the Distribution Department).

Tom had just come from a meeting with the vice president to whom he reported and was at his wits end about the chronic problems in his department and how he could "ever in a million years please all those nurses."

From my meetings with employees prior to starting the management education I knew that support services was a big issue in the organization and the biggest bottlenecks happened to be in Tom's department, according to the nurse managers and employees with whom I had talked. They complained that they had been talking about these problems for several years and that nothing ever seemed to change. As a result, nursing department employees had learned to "work around the system." Nurses were stockpiling essential supplies so they could be certain to have what they most needed for patients. This, of course, added to the problems in Materials Management with inaccurate patient charges and incomplete inventory control.

Tom had asked to meet with me to see if I had "any ideas from other places" and also to vent his frustration and defend his department. As we talked I noticed that he had a hard time staying on the topic at hand and seemed to be going from one issue to another as he "ventilated" his frustrations (deficient Earth). His voice had a whiney, sing-song sound to it (deficient Earth) and I found myself reacting negatively to his "neediness" and wondering how he had remained in this position when he was so obviously overwhelmed (deficient Earth). When I asked about his efforts to problem solve the situation (Fire to support deficient Earth) Tom reported that he had worked with several of the nurse managers to try and improve the delivery of supplies and equipment to their units, but he "just couldn't please any of them." He described his staff as feeling overworked and frustrated, and he echoed their sentiments when asked about his own quality of work life (deficient Earth).

Tom also complained about his weight gain and lack of energy and made it clear that his wife and children were not happy with the "daylight to dark" schedule he had been maintaining for the last year. While complaining of long hours he was unable to articulate any accomplishments in the department in terms of improved systems or better outcomes (deficient Earth). While Tom never actually verbalized his job insecurity, it was obvious that he was worried about losing his job since the vice president to whom he reported was, as he put it, "on my case."

When I asked for more details about systems in place for handling calls, standards for the delivery of supplies, staff turnover rates or data to reflect department response times, his repeated reply was, "We are working on that." He expressed feelings of inadequacy and was obviously getting uncomfortable as the conversation progressed so I suggested that we meet later that afternoon to give me some time to process all the information he had given me.

Energy Assessment

As I left his office I couldn't help but reflect on the irony of being in the "distribution" department surrounded by supplies, carts, and equipment with a director and employees who were obviously feeling "stuck." The deficiency in Earth energy was clear as I thought about all that I had seen and felt in my meeting with him and heard from the earlier staff focus group. The more obvious manifestations included:

- Lack of systems for service delivery
- Employees and director feeling overworked, low morale
- Lack of self-care, weight gain, sense of futility and inadequacy
- Whiney, needy tone of voice
- Sense of being "stuck" or hopeless
- Focus on trying to please and keep everybody happy

Self-Assessment

I purposely took a walk after lunch and found some quiet time to reflect on our conversation. My initial response to Tom's neediness and whiney tone had been negative and I had to remind myself that I was there to help and had a professional obligation to at least make suggestions that could possibly improve the situation. I recognized a desire to rescue and fix, which was a clue for me to monitor my own Earth energy and maintain the boundaries appropriate for a consultant. I had to caution myself to avoid the temptation to solve the problem and instead support the Directors in dealing with the issues. Taking this time to notice my reactions, adjust my attitude, and, most importantly, shift my energy (by removing myself from the energy in the department) proved to be beneficial in our meeting that afternoon.

Intervention

Since the imbalance in Earth energy was obvious I began our meeting by empathizing with Tom that my intent was to be supportive. I told him about experiences in dealing with issues similar to his in another tertiary care medical center and stressed the need to problem solve (Fire) issues in a more effective way rather than trying to "please everybody." I showed Tom an approach to problem solving for use in groups and mentioned that we would be going over the model in class the following day. I suggested that we use one of his department's issues then and he agreed to think about this overnight. In class the next day, as we worked with the problem solving model, Tom and his group developed an action plan. Tom seemed amazed that they had come up with a workable plan in just an hour. We talked about his teaching this model to his employees in their next staff meeting and made plans for him to call and update me after this meeting.

Our next conversation had a more hopeful tone so I knew that improving the problem solving efforts (Fire to feed deficient Earth) had been helpful. Tom's employees had been enthusiastic about actually getting a plan developed to deal with issues and we discussed a structure (Wood) he could use to involve his staff in problem solving with the nurse managers. Based on previous experience, I helped him see the value of working with one or two nurse managers with whom he could begin to develop a sense of teamwork (Fire). I recommended that they represent their collective group rather than his having to field several calls each day. Tom agreed to select two managers who could work with his staff on problem solving and would have a meeting to prioritize the issues (Fire) prior to my returning for another education session the next month.

His demeanor in the subsequent training session was quite different than in our initial meeting—he was like a different person. There was a light in his eyes and enthusiasm in his voice as he told me about the first meeting of his "service coordinating council." Tom was especially pleased to describe an easing in tension with his vice president (now that he could demonstrate progress) and also reported that he was "now leaving here at a decent time" every day, for which both he and his family were grateful.

The course content we were discussing that day proved to augment the (Fire to feed Earth) intervention he had implemented. We reviewed various ways to monitor progress in achieving outcomes and discussed the value of posting information to keep staff informed on their progress.

Tracking outcomes (Earth) was a new concept for him and several of his peers, and Tom decided to talk this over with his council in their next meeting. In a phone call a few weeks later he said how he had graphed the group's progress using bar graphs on his computer and that this was being shared by the nursing representatives in their group meetings as well as in his staff meetings. A game plan (Wood) and the added structure of visually tracking progress (Wood) was clearly supporting the problem solving and team effort (Fire). I suggested that he take members of his council to a similar facility in a nearby city to see systems they had in place (Earth) and learn of their "best practices." Tom liked this idea and we both agreed this would be a nice perk for those who had invested so much time and energy in the group's progress thus far. He later related that this time away as a work group had made a real difference in the way the group worked together—"Less us and them...more we," as he described it. Tom was particularly pleased his vice president agreed to the purchasing of computer software, used in this nearby facility, which greatly improved the Materials Department's monitoring of inventory, a long-standing issue.

In his course evaluation following the last class day, Tom reflected on his learning in the course and credited the module, "Group problem solving/tracking outcomes," with saving his job and quite possibly his marriage!

Looking back on this experience I am reminded again of the value of removing myself from the situation and taking the time to assess and adjust my own energy. Had I not taken that "time out" and regained perspective, I feel certain that my frustration would have been obvious and made Tom feel even more inadequate than he was already feeling at the time of our first meeting. I can see in this experience how attending to the parent element (Fire) with the education and training in problem solving and prioritizing the issues fed the child element (Earth), resulting in improved service and measurable outcomes. The group naturally moved on to the evaluation of their efforts (Metal) without any prompting, and this let me know that the interventions I had chosen were appropriate.

Summary

Healthy Earth energy provides stability in our lives and a level of useful practicality. The routines of everyday life nourish and give us energy for our journey—whether this nourishment takes the form of healthy food, exercise, and meditative quiet time, or whether we feel a sense of support from a manager who makes sure we have what we need to do our job well. On whatever level this sense of stability occurs it is essential for our overall sense of well-being.

"The power of Earth calls us home...that place inside where we feel centered and balanced, at peace with the world."[7]

Metal—
Purity with an Edge

Jennifer Jenkins

Cleaning out a cluttered drawer
The breathtaking translucence of the sun shining
through autumn leaves
The memories of a loved one
An exquisite piece of art
The loss of a job
A simple truth
The catharsis of tears.

We all have experienced the simple and majestic power of Metal energy. It is the essence of what is important and meaningful. It is what sustains us as we experience transitions to new adventures and experiences. It is the core of our beliefs and being. It inspires us to do more and be better. It can bring us to our knees, literally and figuratively. But it also can raise us to new heights of sensation, achievement, and fulfillment.

Metal Energy

Autumn is the season of metallic energy. Table 8-1 summarizes and provides an overview. This time of contraction and preparation for winter is reflected in both our personal and professional lives. In the business cycle, it is when healthy companies reflect on their mission, decisions, communication, and outcomes. The culmination of this evaluation is a more streamlined and effective organization. Linked to a sound process of continuous quality improvement, the evaluation of a company results in deciding what is carried on in the next phase of the cycle and what is discarded. By doing this, the company frees up resources (Water energy) to fuel new directions.

Table 8-1: Metal Energy Overview

Season	Autumn
Color	White
Voice Tone	Weeping, Breathy
Emotion	Grief
Organs	Lungs, Large intestine
Motivation	To evaluate
Thought Process	Evaluation
Personality Type	Artist

In its healthiest manifestations, Metal energy is characterized by a calm, measured approach. Individuals are accepting because they recognize that inherent truths lie in every situation and they are determined to "mine" those truths, even when buried. The word "inspirational" best describes the effective Metal energy individual.

The connection between Water and Metal energy is critical. Literally, the ability of the organization (organism) to continue the cycle is dependent upon making the shift from Metal to Water, from distilling the essence of the organization to defining new directions (rebirth). In Metal the sense of "being on the edge" is the emotional expression. Tears and grief are common. With a cycle ending and a need to let go of some things, most feel certain sadness. A sense of saving the best and getting to take it with you gives individuals a "lighter load" and more energy to confront new directions.

The lungs and large intestine are the organs governing Metal. They represent the natural activity of extracting the last of the essential elements before the waste is eliminated. The large intestine must decide what is essential to life, what is not necessary or even what is toxic. Imbalance in this function leads to diarrhea, constipation, abdominal pain or cramping. Proper bowel functioning makes room in the body. As a result the lungs can inspire fully and cleanse the circulating blood. The skin and mucous membranes can perspire and rid the body of wastes.

The process of inspiration draws one up. In healthy Metal posture is upright and gestures are restrained yet powerful movements. "Less is more" is the operative phrase.

Movements are deliberate, but unlike Wood, they are flexible and free. Individuals with unhealthy Metal energy may be constrained in movement, and either tight or so loose that they do not know what is appropriate behavior or activity for a particular situation.

In keeping with the purification theme, the color of Metal is white. Metal is noted in a whitish hue to the area around the eyes and mouth. In balance, this has a translucent quality; in imbalance the color is dull and even muddy. The skin has a sharp, pungent odor, not unlike the scent of old coins.

Signs of Imbalance

One danger inherent in any energy is its ability to become too enamored with itself. People and groups that thrive in Metal energy can take themselves, the organization, and life far too seriously. They begin to isolate themselves in "ivory towers" and think that they have all the answers or that they are above reproach. They begin to believe that their approach to quality is the right approach and anything different or less is simply unacceptable. This perfectionistic viewpoint is intimidating to others and not helpful in a world where perfection is impossible to achieve. In this situation the use of the Shen cycle may be in order (see page 4). By applying the controlling energy of Fire, Metal can be softened, molded, and made responsive. Communication, prioritization, and humor ensure that Metal types share the evaluative findings, identify what is most important to concentrate on, and help keep enough levity in the situation to prevent the destructive and often cutting impact of Metal on the system (see Table 8-2).

Table 8-2: Metal Energy in Work Groups/Organizational Life

Characteristics Indicating Balance	Characteristics Indicating Imbalance
Have clear, effective evaluations	Has no clear evaluation process
Set and maintain high standards	Intolerant of mediocrity
"Walk the talk" of values	Evidences lack of meaning
Eliminate what is of no value	Demoralized
	Hanging onto the past
	Excessive grieving or inability to grieve

Deficient Metal energy often appears in an inappropriate or extreme reaction to closure or letting go of issues. In some instances, the individual is unable to let go of a relationship even though it is clearly no longer healthy or sustaining and may actually be destructive. Grieving loss is often prolonged and, in some cases, never fully accepted. At the other extreme, a relationship may be left at the first sign of trouble when it is perceived to be more problem than it is worth.

In the organization these imbalances manifest themselves in similar ways. During difficult financial times, a service or department can be perceived to be too costly and, without a careful evaluation of potential ramifications, an announcement will come that the service is being eliminated. In one system this happened to the Home Health Agency. Although financially this department was doing very well, during a difficult financial downturn system administrators were seeking to eliminate any unnecessary services. The cost of running this department was significant and, as a result, the department was summarily eliminated without fanfare. Not many months later, the financial officer of the system realized that this critical service had provided a buffer for the acute care side of the business by providing patients needed services so they could be discharged, avoiding unnecessarily prolonged hospitalizations. Furthermore, the revenue produced by the Home Health Agency enhanced the overall financial position of the system. Both of these benefits were lost because of a hasty decision to close the service without a true evaluation of its benefits.

An over-reliance on tradition and "the way things are done around here" is another manifestation of Metal imbalance. Often evaluation of traditions and approaches for their continued efficacy is simply not done. Instead, the patterns and processes continue, although they may be hopelessly outdated. Holding onto the past makes it very difficult for people and the organization to move into the future. In one organization, people continued to talk about the "good old days" before the merger. When asked when the merger had occurred, it was twenty years previous! People were still clinging to the way things were. This is a clear signal that they had not proceeded through a natural, healing grief process, but instead "got stuck" in the transition from Metal to Water energy.

Organizations with deficient Metal energy exhibit confusion about their true values. Although most health care organizations claim to be mission-driven with a strong focus on service to people in their community, in today's turbulent business environment, it appears that the financial bottom line is what is truly valued. Many teams and systems have completed the work of defining their core values, yet fail to live up to these values on a day-to-day basis. Instead incongruity exists between the rhetoric and the behavior. Thus the quality improvement effort becomes just a "program" in the organization rather than a fully integrated way of providing service and doing business. People in the organization can clearly articulate the values of the organization and its programs, but fail to see the incongruity when their behavior fails to match the stated values.

Figure 8-1: Developmental/Shen Cycle

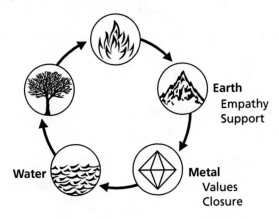

Metal Energy in Review

Metal energy is the seat of our values and beliefs. It sustains us and helps us deal with closure in our lives, ever moving us toward the new direction of Water energy. Energies having a direct impact on Metal are Earth (its mother energy in the Cycle of Creation), Fire (its controlling energy in the K'o cycle), and Water (its child energy). Figures 8-1 and 8-2 summarize these relationships. Depending upon whether an individual or group is experiencing balance, excess or depletion of an energy, one or more of these energies can be used to restore or maintain balance.

Figure 8-2: K'o or Control Cycle

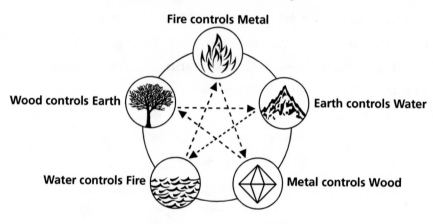

Normally, Earth energy expresses itself with stability, nourishment, and sustenance. This energy prepares the individual or group for introspection and evaluation. By creating a strong, sustainable energy, Earth supports with confidence the evaluation process. People and groups who know that they have built a solid system have no fear about evaluation. They know that the process of sifting through accomplishments and failures encourages a general "house-cleaning" of values, plans, systems, and communications. This evaluation leads to discarding whatever gets in the way of excellence and continued viability. What is left is the core of what makes success. By weeding out what is not helpful and what may be harmful, energy can be given to recognizing success, reinforcing its importance, and using that to fuel new initiatives. Thus Earth energy is the "parent" energy for Metal.

Likewise, a successful evaluation process allows for a focus on what makes success possible. This emphasis on the positive fuels the move to Water (the child). Even an evaluation that uncovers some failures is an opportunity for learning and growth. Organizations and individuals that use failure as a growth opportunity usually find better ways to thrive. They convert a negative outcome into positive energy, which further fuels the transition to Water's new directions and identifies new resources to support Water.

Case Study

Prior to the intervention, I had been working with this client off and on for more than a year. The health care organization was implementing a new decision-making model for the organization. In this model, more authority for decisions was being moved to the departmental level, both for administrative and clinical matters. They were about two-thirds of the way through their implementation. Having been housed in a very old building, they had built a modern new facility designed to bring care providers closer to the clients they served and help support their new decision-making model. The new facility would group services to better serve the clients.

Externally, changes in reimbursement, delivery of community-wide services, and lifestyle changes of the citizens were having a dramatic impact on the number of clients being served in the organization. Many previously served clients were now being cared for in short-stay units and ambulatory surgical and clinical facilities, and through home health and community services. The need to conserve resources, improve efficiency and productivity, and redesign systems was essential for the survival of this organization (as it is in similar organizations across the country).

As a result, several smaller patient care units were being asked to combine and work together as one new group on a larger physical unit. The clash of cultures was inevitable. For some the process was managed successfully. For others, the process was painful, wrenching, and undesirable. That morning, I walked into the latter.

Energy Assessment

I was to meet with part of the staff of the two units at 7:30 a.m. and again at 3:30 p.m. This would allow time for members of all three shifts to meet. Those not scheduled for the day had been asked to come in during either one of the meeting times. I had been warned that these two departments were not handling the transition well. Supervisors expressed dismay at the level of apathy, hostility, grief, and general lack of cooperation expressed by a large percentage of the employees.

Only one of the two unit directors would be kept. The two groups had cared for somewhat different groups of clients: one for children, the other for adults, yet neither group wanted to accept leadership from someone from the "other side." There was genuine concern that the quality of care was being compromised, which was at least partially borne out in a recent rise in incident reports and medication errors.

I was known to the employees on both units and had enjoyed an open and frank dialogue with them in the past. They had not hesitated in sharing their concerns and usually listened with courtesy and respect, even if they disagreed with my comments.

Initial Impressions

At 7:30 a.m., when the first meeting was scheduled, only three people were ready to begin. It took the director fifteen minutes to round up everyone and get them in the room. Many hung back and sat in chairs just outside the room, often with the chairs turned at least partially away from the others and me. Others crowded close.

As I waited for people to assemble, I heard many muted, breathy, even "choking" voices. There did not seem to be enough air for all of them to breathe deeply. I also heard voices that had a "shouting" quality—forceful and angry, though not really loud. A few "singing" voices could be heard comforting others. Some voices seemed to "moan." Lackluster and droning in quality, these voices seemed without hope. I heard no laughter or gaiety.

Looking around the room, most were sitting at the edge of their chairs or slumped, with their backs rounded and their heads nearly touching the chair backs. I felt that only the friction of their clothes against the chairs kept them from flowing out onto the floor—perhaps down the hall and out of the facility itself (Water). Others were sitting more upright, but shoulders were slumped forward as though they were protecting their insides, their core (Metal). A few were more rigid and upright (Wood). Many were solidly in their chairs, looking as though they were a part of the chair itself. Their center of gravity was right in the middle. I did not have a sense that they could move; it was as if they were an immovable mountain daring me to move them (Earth). A couple of people were jumping up and down, both waving their arms to get everyone seated, trying to get people together in groups where they would be comfortable (Fire). I knew this was going to be a challenge!

As we began, I noted tears, disagreements, sadness, apathy, and even a little defiance. As the meeting continued, anger, hopelessness, fear, grief, and sympathy were expressed in words, actions, and feelings.

Phrases caught my attention as a barometer of the group's feelings. "I will miss my friends" (Metal/Fire); "The quality of care is being compromised" (Metal); "No one in the office cares what happens to us/our patients" (Earth/Metal); "I don't see why we have to do this" (Wood); "We can't do this; we don't have enough staff and those we have don't have the skills" (Water/Metal); "It will never be the same" (Metal). I listened for recurring themes, intensity (or lack of it), and behaviors supporting or contradicting the feelings being expressed in the words.

The Five Energies in Action

As in most situations, I found all energies present. Some were more strongly expressed, some were very muted, but all were present. By correlating behavior, content of what was said, sounds, and emotions, I determined the state of Metal energy, the deficiencies in Earth and Water, and the fact that Fire was nearly missing.

A majority of the group was sitting fairly upright in a closed position, as though they were protecting themselves. Their voices had a tremulous quality and tears often flowed. They frequently made comments that were critical of coworkers, the quality of care, and their supervisors/administrators. Moreover, they usually positioned themselves and their former unit as the one that really cared and gave good care. They described themselves in self-pitying terms. They talked about the need for rules (the ones they had on their previous unit) and the need for rigid policies and procedures, and they generally lacked flexibility in thinking or behavior.

The afternoon group seemed even more closed in body language. These people also had a tremulous voice quality and many cried openly. They were quieter. When pressed, they usually voiced the same things that had already been said. It was as though they took the shape of the dominant energy/voices in the room. They usually reacted to any criticism as though personally attacked and wounded. Both of these groups were indicative of Metal energy: The morning an excess, the afternoon a deficiency.

A significant number, though not the majority, in the afternoon group expressed a real sense of fear. They temporarily would respond to someone's idea, only to dissolve into concern and fear that their jobs were in real danger. Like Metal types, their arms were closed across their bodies, but unlike Metal, they slid low in the chair. Their voices droned on, making me think of water slowly wearing away stone. Their energy seemed to drown any spark of enthusiasm from others. I noticed that many of these people seemed inordinately tired and had dark circles under their eyes. They were nearly all sloppily dressed and some looked as though they had not washed their clothes in some time. Though clearly sad, this segment did not cry, as though they were too dry and cried out. This was deficient Water energy.

A small number of staff remained glued to their chairs. Most were clearly overweight and filled the space of the chair. Several had brought sugary pastries for their breakfast. Their main contribution, often in a singsong voice, was, "The administration needs to be more caring," or, "Nobody cares" what is happening to them, to the patients, to the hospital. These individuals, more than their colleagues, seemed to need the approval of others, for they frequently asked, "Don't you see what I mean?" Their solutions nearly always included the addition of food (potluck dinners, meetings around mealtimes, etc.). This deficient Earth energy contributed to the lack of inertia of the group.

Three people were blatantly angry. Their voices shouted, if not in volume, then most certainly in quality and harshness. They sat or stood upright and gestured with sharp, staccato-like movements, pointing their fingers at others or the world in general. Their ideas were expressed quickly without a clear appreciation for the consequences. Their comments were frequently insensitive.

In addition, two people sat so rigidly that I thought if I touched them they would shatter. They did not speak often and when they did they were irritable yet unable to express why. Though clearly tired, they held themselves upright as if they would disintegrate if they relaxed. This group expressed a deficiency in Wood energy while the former, angry group expressed excess.

I also noted two individuals on opposite sides of the room who seemed to be opposites of each other. One person was clearly manifesting manic behaviors. Jumping up to get another chair for someone, fidgeting in her chair, impatient with those expressing negative feelings, she laughed inappropriately and seemed more intent on drawing attention to herself rather than on really hearing what her coworkers were concerned about. Her excess Fire was contrasted with her colleague across the room, who seemed totally burned out. There was no spark in her eyes and she seemed isolated from everyone else in the room. Several times she seemed disconnected from the conversation and appeared to be "somewhere else." Her deficient Fire was reflected in the ashen color of her face.

Metal Assessment Tips for the Novice

Energy is expressed in many ways and each individual will be quicker to pick up on some things than others will. Effectively using the Five Element model requires learning to be comfortable with at least two or three manifestations so you can check yourself and increase the accuracy of your assessment.

For example, a droning or groaning voice may indicate excessive Water energy. It may also point to a deficient Fire energy, in which laughter and joy are drowned out by overwhelming situations that diminish resources needed to keep life's Fire burning, especially if a chronic lack of resources exists. If you hear the groaning voice and the person is slumped in his chair and has dark circles under his eyes and is eating salty pretzels, a Water imbalance is the likely assessment.

In assessing Metal imbalances, look for congruency in at least three of the following:

- **Emotion**—sad, grieving; tears easily—or never
- **Voice**—weepy (as though about to cry), breathy (like an inspirational speaker)
- **Activity**—most active very early in the morning (may get up between 3 a.m. and 7 a.m.)
- **Posture**—Sits or stands tall (as though suspended or pulled by a rope attached to the chest)
- **Gestures**—restrained, but up and out (hands often shoulder level or higher)
- **Smell**—metallic, or fresh raw flesh or fish
- **Season**—loves autumn and is energized during that time
- **Geographic preferences**—prefers the desert or the West, where it is dry and not humid
- **Complaints**—may complain of suffering from allergies, lower gastrointestinal complaints, skin conditions, dry scalp or skin
- **Humor**—has a cutting edge (when healthy, it may be insightful; when unhealthy it will likely be sadistically sarcastic and hurtful)
- **Color**—whitish hue around eyes and mouth; often dresses in white or metallic colors

The important part of accurate assessments is not that you become an expert at seeing all of these. What is important is to assess several parameters and to look for patterns over time. Remember that anyone can express any energy in excess or deficiency at different points in time. When the expressions repeat themselves and/or develop a recognizable pattern, then you can be more certain of the validity of the assessment.

Assessing My Own Energy

In this particular case study, I had some prior knowledge of the groups and individuals involved. Knowing the organizational framework and the style of leadership at both the executive and department level, I further anticipated how the group might respond. I knew that how I expressed (or did not express) my own energy would have an impact on the group. It was imperative that I assess myself before going into the meeting, and also frequently during the meeting. Each of us has some energies with which we resonate more easily—some positively, others negatively. I needed to be aware of my own responses so that I did not influence the group in non-productive ways.

I arrived on the unit about fifteen minutes early to assess the meeting space. It was a small room with one door. I decided to sit just two or three seats from the door to be sure my energy would not be confined if I felt trapped by the group. I then went to a quiet room alone to spend five minutes visualizing the meeting and how it would unfold. I envisioned a full range of expressions from individuals and attempts to drain my energy from me since I anticipated some depletion. I decided to draw upon my Earth energy and went into the meeting centered and respectful of my own limitations and the rights and needs of others. I sat comfortably and relaxed, hoping to convey strength and stability, comfort and options.

As the meeting unfolded, I frequently and consciously paid attention to my own energy. I turned toward speakers and gave them my full attention. I maintained a calm voice and concerned demeanor. I made sure that I remained upright, but relaxed. At one point I felt myself irritated by the often scathing comments. I simply readjusted my position, relaxing muscles that had tensed, and chose to respond in a warm, non-judgmental voice. A little later when the group's energy was beginning to mobilize, I found an opportunity to use some light humor (K'o cycle for Fire to control Metal). At the end of the meeting, I asked everyone to rise together to shift energy upward and prepared them to move forward. I did this once I felt the group's energy had come together so my energy would be connected to theirs. Too soon and they would have felt betrayed.

Interventions

As I prepared for this intervention, I paid close attention to the following wisdom.

1. I would need to conserve my own energy to be able to help the group (my comfort in Earth and Metal can make me vulnerable in situations where these elements are depleted).

2. The Metal to Water transition is perhaps the most critical to survival of the organization (without closure and new beginnings, the entity stagnates and dies).

3. With depletion of an energy state, progress would need to be measured and limited—no "save the world" strategies here.

My goal for the meeting was to help the individuals become united around some guiding principle or mission so the newly merged department could move in new directions (Water). The group was clearly mourning the loss of identity of two distinct departments as they were being merged into one. The majority of individuals exhibited classic Metal energy signs, mostly deficient. With the additional assessment that Metal's parent energy, Earth, was also depleted, I felt that working in Metal too soon would further drain the energy of the group. I elected to begin my intervention in Earth energy to mobilize the group's Earth energy so they had the strength to transition from Metal to Water.

Accordingly, as soon as the meeting was called to order, using a softly melodious voice, I said, "It must be hard to lose your separate departments; I know it would make me very sad. It strikes me that we need to make time to celebrate what each employee liked about the individual departments and share that with each other. It important that each department knows what was good and what you are taking a chance on losing by combining these departments."

The impact was immediate. Tears flowed as the first of many individuals began to share their feelings of loss and sadness or as they celebrated their successes on their respective units:

"I will miss my unit so much; we had such a good team."
"We worked so hard to build the unit staff and foster team spirit; we were just beginning to see the positive results."

"We had finally worked out work schedules that seemed to fit everyone's lifestyle."

"I loved working with the others on my shift; I don't know the people on the other unit and I am not sure we will work together so well."

"I loved taking care of the children. We really worked to make it a positive experience for the children and families."

"Our unit director was the best. We are concerned that the organization will not value her contribution and find a good position for her."

The comments went on for ten or fifteen minutes. As the sharing unfolded, I noticed a shift in energy. Individuals were reaching out to touch others and hold hands. Tissues were offered and pats on the back or hugs. Significantly these were often exchanged between members of the two different units. Earth energy was mobilizing. It was time to shift into Metal.

I sat up a little more, remaining flexible and open. Adjusting my voice to a breathier quality, I said, "It is clear that there is much to be proud of in each of the units. Further, many examples shared by one group were also seen as positive examples by the other group. It reminds me of a funeral. Most everyone comes saddened, but with differing memories. Throughout the eulogy and the gathering of friends and family at the house later, stories and memories are shared. Soon it is evident that there are many themes that emerge from the varying stories. As each person leaves that day, they will take with them new or revised truths about their loved one. These expressions will change how each person goes about their life and how they will relate with other friends and family."

Looking around the room, I saw that I had their attention. Most had pulled themselves more upright. I noticed that there was more movement and less rigidity in postures. Now was the time for them to test their Metal energy. I asked, "What have you heard today that is clearly one of the values you want to retain on the new unit?"

"Caring."

"Quality of care."

"Respect."

"Compassion."

"Flexibility."

"Trust."

The answers came quickly, succinctly. Heads nodded in agreement. No one seemed closed or negative about any of the values being expressed. We captured all of these on flip chart paper and hung them up for all to see.

I used mind-mapping technique and put the new unit in the middle with the word "Values" and placed the values expressed in spokes radiating from the center (see Figure 8-3). Mind mapping is an excellent tool to keep themes in front of the group so they stay focused on the work at hand.

Figure 8-3: Mind-Map

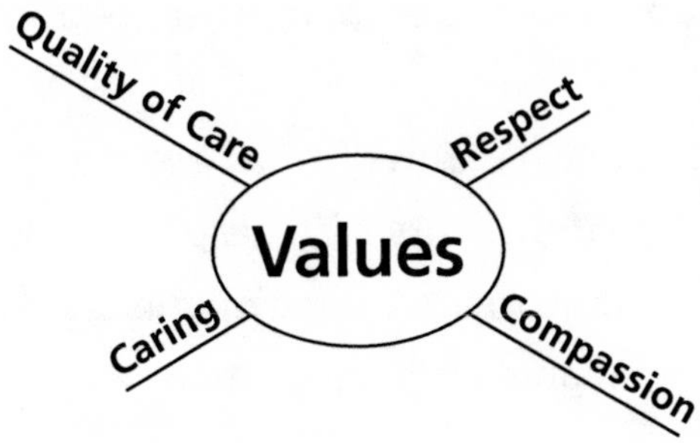

Soon one of the members of the group jumped up and asked to record items for me. Her enthusiasm was matched by the group calling out more values and things seemed to move almost too quickly. Suddenly laughter was heard and several shared a humorous story with the group about doing a similar exercise on their unit a year ago. The upshot of the story was that their group had so many values they almost got overwhelmed. What they found humorous was that after they discussed them and eliminated those that were similar, what seemed an overwhelming sixteen values had been reduced to five. The laughter and story (Fire energy) further energized the group (remember the K'o cycle in which Fire controls excess Metal).

We then began to discuss the various values on the mind map. Comments become more and more insightful. There was a real sense that the boundaries of the old departments had blurred. Comments were offered in support of another's position. Disagreements were thoughtful, not hurtful. We were close. I elected not to say anything for a few minutes. Everyone reflected on the list and I could see the seeds of imagination stirring. I asked for someone to summarize in one short statement what the mission should be for the new unit. It was quiet for another few minutes. I waited, knowing that the shift from Metal to Water requires quiet reflection, thought, and stillness. Truths are often deep and must be brought slowly to the surface.

Then someone ventured a suggestion: "Our unit will deliver compassionate, quality care, respecting the rights of the patient and fellow coworkers." For a moment, no one moved or spoke. Then several spoke up. Now there was excitement and assent. A few offered refinements, which were debated by the group. Some words were added, others changed, and a few deleted. The mission read:

Our mission is to provide compassionate, high quality care to patients and families. We recognize the rights of patients to control their own care and to be given the information and training to make informed decisions. We believe that this care is best delivered when we respect the rights of coworkers, support their ongoing education and training, and when we incorporate ongoing performance improvement strategies in our daily work.

Again, silence. Then laughter, smiles, hugs. They agreed to elect a new unit clinical practice committee to carry on the work of implementing this mission. A person was appointed to put together an election committee. I congratulated them on their success. No one wanted to leave. This group of individuals, who could barely come together an hour ago, now did not want to leave. They had made the shift from Metal to Water. With coaching and support they would be successful.

Lessons Learned

Perhaps what was reinforced most in this intervention was to have patience and look for the least intervention to cause the greatest energetic shift. With my nature to "push or pull" things, it is tempting to use a stronger, quicker intervention than what is usually needed. What this interaction reinforced is that when energy is prematurely or forcefully pushed or pulled it often has exactly the opposite effect of what is desired.

To illustrate, in this group, it was clear that they needed to shift energy from Metal to Water so that the new department could move forward. At one point it seemed the group had sufficiently mobilized its Metal energy. Individuals had shared their grief over losing their respective departments, so I asked, "What direction do you want the new unit to take?" Instead of beginning a dialogue about new directions, fresh tears flowed and they retreated into their grief.

I immediately retracted my question and asked again what they remembered about their own unit that made them proud. They immediately began sharing what they felt the essence of both of the departments was. About ten minutes later, one member of the group said, "You know, what is clear to me is that our two units have a lot in common. For example, we both want to be respected, we both want to give quality care, and we both want to be known as the best at what we do."

I could not pull them into a discussion about their new mission (Water) until they had finished their evaluation and wake for their dead units. At that point, they could move themselves. My role in this situation was to give them permission to stay in their energy until they could mobilize their energy enough to move forward.

Summary

Autumn is Metal energy. The days are shorter, the air crisper and cleaner. It sparkles as though filled with tiny crystals reflecting light with the intensity of a lens, focusing it on objects and making them shimmer. The past year is felt deep within the body. There are memories, friends, and projects that are carried forward into a new year, and many that are left behind. Preparing for the coming winter means feeling things will not be the same. There is happiness for having shared so many experiences and optimism that the new year brings experiences to enrich our lives. The season and the energy are about finding the value in those things that have gone before, yet not letting them impede our progress into the new world of our future.

Metal—pure, distilled, sharp edges. It is an essence propelling us in new directions and sustaining us with value. Metal makes room in our lives so we can move to Water energy where new directions continue our growth and forward momentum. Savor the moment, and move on.

9

Applying the Model— Diagnosis and Intervention

Jo Manion and Sharon Cox

N ow that you are beginning to grasp the basics of the Five Element model, perhaps you find yourself wanting to apply these ideas to improve a group process or the outcomes of a project in which you are involved. Something about the simplicity of this model and the way it just seems to make sense causes many to want to jump in and use it at their next team meeting. As we have taught this model to managers, executives, and other consultants, we have come to recognize that typical burst of enthusiasm as "light bulbs go off" for the listener and he or she sees ways to move from just understanding the model to applying it with a group.

While we are gratified each time we see how easily people grasp the beauty and usefulness of the Five Element model, we believe it is important to stress that the use of this ancient wisdom follows certain principles and requires careful thought and intention. The purpose of this chapter is to review those principles and share steps required to use the model in a responsible way. Many of these concepts were referred to in the section on the different energies. This chapter outlines a template of options as well as what to do if the approach attempted does not seem to alleviate the situation.

As we have said, the process of applying the wisdom of the Five Element model to work/life situations is characterized as an intervention. The intervention includes assessing a situation and your own personal energy, choosing appropriate alternatives meant to help or improve the situation, and finally, evaluating outcomes. The intervention process is actually similar to other training a manager might receive. Additional learning on how to run an effective meeting, for example, results in the manager intentionally choosing to do certain things to make meetings more effective.

As we use the Five Element model, we choose to take certain actions to alter energy in keeping with the basic principles inherent in Chinese medicine. Assessing and intervening on group energy requires respect for the sacredness of this ancient wisdom and an understanding of the conditions in which this intervention process occurs. Our belief in the thoughtful nature of this process and the principles involved is what led us to devote an entire chapter to this process. The examples used here to illustrate the intervention process are generally related to work with groups. However, the same principles apply in work with individuals or on a larger scale of organizational development. While the steps in the intervention process may be similar to ones you have used in other situations, there are also some unique features with this model.

The Intervention Process
Step One—Assessment

As with any intervention, the first step involves an assessment process. Since you will be primarily interested in an energy assessment, the process requires additional and different skills than you might otherwise use. The assessment takes into consideration the content of conversations, the tone and character of voices, the posture and behavior of group members, emotions present, and your knowledge of the group's history. As you reflect on how the group functions as a whole, are all five energies— Water, Wood, Fire, Earth, Metal—evident? In your assessment, rather than listening just to the content of discussions, listen to the energy of the voice as well. Is there a shout to the voice or a groan, a laugh, or a weeping sound? What posture is predominant in the group? Are people slumped and floundering in their chair or having difficulty sitting still, flitting from topic to topic? Is one person acting as a "container" for a certain energy, perhaps by taking charge while others just wait for direction? Are group members stressed by multiple priorities and mixed messages? Are they worried about job security and reluctant to speak up for fear of retaliation? Do they laugh easily or do they seem to be devoid of any humor? These are just a few of the ways you can begin to assess the group to determine its energy.

Getting a visual "map" of the group energy is often helpful. Do this by placing the initials of the group member in the circle representing the predominant energy he or she is demonstrating, as illustrated in Figure 9-1. This visual map of group energy will often depict an excess of some energies and a deficiency in others. It is also helpful to observe the group on more than one occasion to see if these behaviors and patterns remain true over time or are situationally based.

Figure 9-1: Energy Map

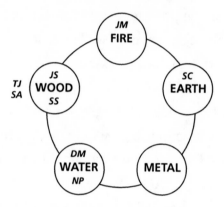

Consider making the assessment process interactive and involving the group members in assessing their own energy. Simply asking the group, "What do you think is going on here?" elicits their ideas and thoughts. Another easy, non-threatening way to create involvement is to have the group draw a picture of how they see things in the organization or in their department. These pictures often reflect the predominant group energy and validate your assessment. If the group is large, divide it into several smaller groups of six or eight people.

Several years ago we worked with a group of managers who were having difficulty forming as a group. They slouched in their chairs each time we met with them and seemed fearful and reluctant to express their feelings. They had no sense of purpose for their meetings and characterized their group as "rudderless." Working in four small groups, they drew pictures expressing how they "saw things in their division," and it was no surprise that all four pictures had a water theme. One depicted a body going down for the third time, another had a ship about to sink, one had people floundering in deep water and trying to find dry land, and the last group depicted themselves as a solitary island being circled by sharks in the water.

One advantage to making part of the assessment process interactive is that the group is more likely to be receptive to intervention if they have participated in the process. Involving the group can be as simple as sharing an observation like, "This group seems to start lots of projects but seldom finishes anything," and listening to hear how this observation resonates with the group. Sharing your observation about the group's energy, as in, "This group seems really down and has low energy today," may be a way of giving the group permission to be honest about how they are feeling. During the assessment, no one should be challenged. Trust is broken when people are afraid their comments and observations are not going to be received well.

* * *

When groups are grappling with highly volatile situations or experiencing intense emotions we can be tempted to react or abbreviate the assessment step. It requires discipline to select an intervention based on the real energy issue within the group. In some cases, it is helpful to call for a break and remove yourself from the situation, even if only briefly, to reflect on the predominant energies being expressed. In a volatile situation it is of utmost importance to assess and adjust your own energy to avoid being pulled into the group's energy.

Step Two—Self-Assessment/Adjust Energy

As we have mentioned, group energy is contagious and therefore it is very important to assess your own energy before intervening in any way with a group's energy. This is easier said than done. All too often we overlook our own contribution to the energy we are observing, inadvertently becoming part of the problem or already deteriorating situation. It is so easy to be drawn into the group's energy and lose our effectiveness without even knowing how it happened. Assessing energy is a two-way street. If you only observe the group, you are working with one-half of the energy picture. Taking the time for a thoughtful and honest self-assessment is one of the key factors in the intervention process. A certain degree of self-awareness is pivotal to being effective with the Five Element model. In what energies are you most comfortable? Which energies are difficult for you to deal with? The answers to these questions offer insight into your strengths or vulnerabilities in dealing with certain kinds of energy.

For example, an experienced facilitator, Irene, found herself in a situation with a newly formed team whose members were exhibiting intense negativity and anger. Irene had a warm, gregarious style and was accustomed to winning over groups with her charismatic nature (Fire energy). Noting the group's negativity, Irene intensified her expansive, joyful style. This proved to be ineffective. She found herself getting increasingly frustrated with the group's negativity and on the verge of responding to them in an angry and critical way—being drawn into their energy. The last thing they needed was more Wood energy given the excess amount they were exhibiting. She decided to call a ten-minute break and found a quiet spot where she could regroup. As Irene reflected on the group's energy, she knew she needed to adjust her energy and change her approach.

Clearly the group was in excessive Wood energy and struggling with ways to deal with their differences. Irene felt herself being drawn into their energy and losing her patience. The last thing they needed was more Wood energy! As Irene reflected on her observations of the group, she knew she needed to adjust her energy and change her approach. After the break she reconvened the group and used a more reflective and thoughtful energy with them (Metal), which allowed them to feel they were being heard. Their energy shifted when they felt heard and they were able to move on with a productive meeting. Responding to them in their own energy would have made a difficult situation almost beyond repair.

Susan, a manager working with her team in a planning retreat, provides another example of the need to notice and adjust one's own energy. Susan is an enthusiastic, cheerleader kind of person (Fire energy) with lots of ideas and high energy. The members of her team had experienced a productive year but they were voicing some concerns about their ability to maintain such a hectic pace over the long term. Susan had initiated this planning retreat to help the team focus and set priorities so it would feel less fragmented. Susan later related that she had to be very aware of her own energy and influence on the group throughout the day. Because they enjoyed being together in a retreat setting and had fun brainstorming ideas for new projects (Fire energy), she had to make a conscious effort to manage her own natural Fire energy so that she did not get caught up in all the fun and fail to stay on task. She chose to use a Wood energy approach, focusing on a "vital few" projects with time frames attached and specific responsibilities delineated. Later in the day, when the plan was well developed, the group celebrated their work with some fun. Taking the time to notice and adjust her own energy made an enormous difference in Susan's ability to effectively facilitate the group.

We mentioned earlier that self-awareness is important in working with this model. To be effective in working with groups or in organizational development, insight into your own strengths and vulnerabilities using the Five Element model is crucial. It is important to have a sense of your own basic energy since that always enters the picture when working with groups. Beinfeld and Korngold offer descriptions of the elements to determine, at least in a broad sense, one's own energy type. In explaining the basic energy we are born with, they write:

> We have styles of being in the world, inclinations and gifts akin to the five seasons...within each of us there is a particular phase around which the others spin, the source of our deepest impulses...this phase is our type. By learning how we are "put together," our nature is revealed. When we know ourselves, we can behave accordingly...informed about our virtues and

frailties, helping us to be wiser in our choices about what to pursue and what to avoid.[1]

There may be times when your assessment of the group's energy leads to the realization that you are not the best person to work with a particular group. Or your assessment may indicate the need to bring in another person who has more ease in dealing with a particular energy to co-facilitate. We observed a good example of this in a highly experienced educator/presenter who was asked to co-present a session on "Managing Transitions" for employees in an organization experiencing tremendous change. The presenter, Ron, had been a successful football coach in his past and his predominant energy was, not surprisingly, Fire. His high-intensity, expansive, and joyful Fire energy just did not fit the assignment of working with people experiencing a grief reaction to the changes in their world. When participants failed to respond to him, Ron's instinct was to become even more dynamic and enthusiastic, trying even harder to draw people out.

Taking the time to do a thoughtful energetic assessment of a situation as well as the strengths and liabilities we bring to the situation is part of our responsible use of this model. Acupuncturists often speak of the need to honor a person's energy and treat him or her with the intention of helping rather than manipulating a person's energy. We need to honor the group's energy and thoughtfully help the situation. In this regard, the Five Element model serves as both a group diagnostic tool and a template for self-evaluation and intervention.

Step Three—Choose an Intervention

Select an intervention using your knowledge of the group's energy, an awareness of your own energy, and an understanding of the principles of energy presented in Chapter 3. As you consider the options you have for crafting an intervention, keep in mind the operating guideline used by the Chinese when they are considering the appropriateness of an intervention— the Law of Least Action.

The Law of Least Action means the less you do, the better. Interventions should be as minimal as possible, as in a few well-chosen words, so that the group can find its own capacity and you are not using more energy than the situation warrants. This is in keeping with a principle used by consultants in the field of organizational development referred to as "less is more."[2] Connelly also describes this principle as she uses acupuncture needles to treat a patient, adding, "The number of needles in any one treatment varies but...the fewer the number of needles used to affect the desired change, the better.[3]

This principle requires a thoughtful assessment of the situation rather than just going with a hunch. It also requires you to keep your ego out of the process and to consider the needs of the group first. Also implied in this principle is a willingness to trust that the process will unfold as it needs to, rather than feeling a need to be in control. The questions, as you work through the assessment process, are: "What are the one or two things I might do to effect the desired change? What are the one or two things that would allow the group to use their own energy more efficiently or wisely?"

Option 1: Energy Is Deficient

If your assessment indicates that a particular element or energy is deficient in the group, your intervention is based on the Shen cycle, or the developmental cycle. It depicts the clockwise flow of energy (see Figure 9-2) and reflects the way in which one element gives rise to the next element. One energy supports the next energy and so on until the cycle completes and begins again. When an energy is deficient, it can be supported by an intervention on the preceding energy. An example of this might be a team having difficulty agreeing on a strategic plan for its department (deficient Wood). A successful intervention would be to have the group revisit its mission statement and available resources (Water). A simple way to remember this approach is, "If the energy is deficient, then feed it," which means intervening on the energy or element preceding the one that is deficient.

Figure 9-2: Development/Shen Cycle

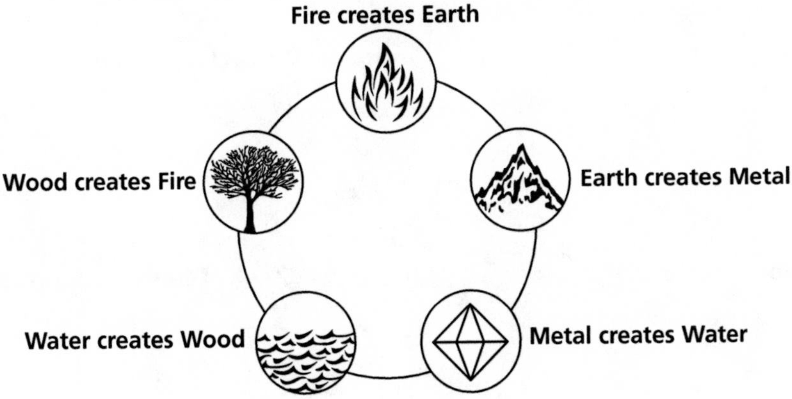

Fire creates Earth

Wood creates Fire

Earth creates Metal

Water creates Wood

Metal creates Water

Option 2: Energy Is Excessive

If the energy in the group is excessive, it can be balanced by using the Control or K'o cycle. As Figure 9-3 illustrates, the Control cycle uses the energy of one element to keep another energy in balance. Water puts out Fire, Fire melts Metal, Metal cuts Wood, Wood pierces and covers the Earth, and Earth holds back Water. In the example of Irene working with the angry group (page 164), she used the K'o cycle to intervene with the group demonstrating excess Wood energy.

Irene chose to adjust her energy and relate to them using Metal energy, since Metal controls Wood. She chose to listen carefully to them, asking key questions about the values they had in common and capitalized on their readiness to let go of things they could not influence. As the group reflected on their values and desires to focus their energies on things that really mattered to them, they agreed to disagree on some issues and moved on. Her ability to listen and ask meaningful questions used Metal energy to balance excessive Wood energy.

Figure 9-3: Control or K'o Cycle

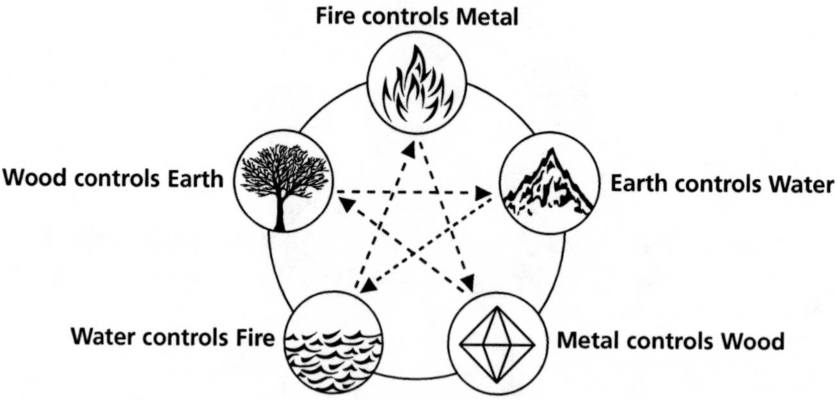

Fire controls Metal

Wood controls Earth

Earth controls Water

Water controls Fire

Metal controls Wood

Another simple and common example occurs when a group meeting has become unfocused and members are getting off-topic. The discussion is far afield from the agenda item being discussed. A helpful strategy is to use a Water energy intervention to bring the group back, for example, by simply asking, "What is the issue here and is it worth using this much of our time discussing it?" Having agenda items identified with a code, such as Discussion, Action or Information, is useful. If this is simply an information item and no decision is anticipated, the group can easily be recalled by pointing this out. Or, the timekeeper may point out how much time has already been expended in discussing the issue and ask the group to make a decision about wise use of its resources (in this case, the group time it has remaining).

Option 3: Fill in a Missing Function

In Chapter 2 we discussed the functions within each element or energy (see Figure 9-4). These functions represent the yin (contained) and the yang (active) aspect of each element. For instance, in the Water element, the yang aspect relates to the function of using resources appropriately while the yin aspect is concerned with a clear sense of mission and purpose. When one of these functions is absent in an element, problems manifest in that energy, since both the yin and yang aspects need to come together for that energy to be balanced. The Chinese refer to the coming together of the two aspects of an energy as the "juncture of yin and yang" and this coming together is necessary for the energy to move to the next element.

Figure 9-4: Five Elements/Twelve Functions

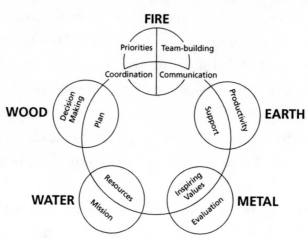

If a function is missing, energy will be blocked and the group remains stuck in that energy. This missing function and stuck energy was obvious in a group that seemed to be continually planning but were never able to make a decision. They were increasingly frustrated (Wood energy) and ready to splinter into factions. When the facilitator offered practical advice on how to make decisions as a group and gave them an opportunity to practice these approaches, they were able to function as a more cohesive group and move on to problem solving and coordination of their projects (Fire energy). This intervention involved offering specific skill sets so that they could fill in a missing function and progress with their development as a team.

Juncture of Yin and Yang—

each element has both yin aspects and yang aspects. When these work in concert, the energy is manifested in a healthy way. Example: In Wood energy, the yin is planning and the yang is decision making. If these two aspects of Wood energy are not in concert, planning might be excessive (analysis paralysis) or there might be "shoot from the hip" decision making.

Option 4: Container of Energy

As you observe the energy in groups you may notice one person monopolizes a function to such an extent that the group comes to rely on him or her rather than bearing responsibility for that function collectively. The energy of that function is contained in one person rather than being dispersed throughout the group. This creates an imbalance in the flow of energy in the group and, in the language of Chinese medicine, this person is acting as a container.

If the group is to function optimally, the energy needs to be present throughout the group, not contained just within one person. For example, a self-appointed spokesperson who speaks for others so that they never have to take a risk or decide what they need keeps the Wood energy (decision making, taking a stand) from developing effectively in the group. Obviously, an effective intervention is to "open up the container" so that the energy is dispersed throughout the group. This can be as simple as saying, "How do the rest of you feel about this issue?"

This imbalance is a common issue at the organizational level as well. When one individual or a select group becomes a container for a certain function or kind of energy, the consequences for both the person who becomes a container and for the organization as a whole can be serious. The person who is the container may be seen as a savior, which is an onerous burden for anyone to carry, or may become a scapegoat if things do not progress as desired. The personal consequence for the individual who serves as a container is that he or she often becomes depleted in the particular energy and eventually leaves the organization. Because the energy has not been developed more fully throughout the system, the loss of the individual then has serious ramifications. That type of energy is essentially lost to the organization unless rapid action is taken to replace it.

An example of this was evident in one Midwestern health care system where the organization's answer to the quality movement was to hire an expert from industry. Tom came into the organization and initiated the Quality Improvement program, pouring heart and soul into the development of the mission and structure, creating a plan and developing relationships within the system. He prepared a group of internal facilitators who, with him, became known as the "quality gurus." They were widely respected and highly skilled at teaching the concepts and facilitating process improvement groups throughout the organization. Several years into this initiative, though, Tom began to feel depleted and burned out. He and his band of facilitators were still "waving the banner," but their efforts were not taking root in the organization. It was clear that the concepts had not been fully assimilated into the culture.

Tom became more and more discouraged and, seemingly unable to communicate the underlying problem in a manner that was constructive, his effectiveness declined further. As with many "programs du jour," once the newness passed, Tom felt support being withdrawn. His behavior and commitment to the organization markedly changed and the breaking point came when he was told his position, which had reported directly to the CEO, would be demoted considerably. In his pain and frustration he did the unforgivable: in the middle of an orientation class with new employees he told them that he no longer believed in what he was teaching or in the organization, and he just walked out! His employment was terminated the same day.

When this situation is analyzed from a Five Element standpoint, Tom had so much ownership for quality (Metal energy) that no one else felt they had to take it on as their own responsibility. While we each have an affinity for certain functions (or energies), like a natural ability to be supportive (Earth) or an ability to see what needs to happen and make a decision (Wood), in a healthy system we do not play that role exclusively. This point is even more obvious in organizations where everyone needs to be concerned with customer service (Earth) or the wise use of financial resources (Water) and not just the employees in those support departments.

Option 5: Balance the Expenditure/Replenishment Cycle

As mentioned in Chapter 3, Wood and Fire elements are considered the expending or yang energies in the cycle. Earth is the transition element to the yin energies of Water and Metal. These last two energies are concerned with replenishing the energy of the cycle. All too often, especially in Western cultures, we allow ourselves to spin out of balance by ignoring the yin side of the cycle. This is often obvious in groups that have multiple projects on the front burner but cannot point to any project they have actually completed. This pattern is often repeated on a larger scale in organizations that pour time and money into research and development (Water and Wood) but have a poor track record for bringing products to market. In the language of the Chinese this is referred to as "perpetual startup." This is also true of the organization with a pattern of multiple, frequent change projects initiated, but never actually anchored in the organizational culture. Over time this pattern exhausts resources and the resulting imbalance is obvious. Attending to the expenditure/replenishment cycle is another way to use the wisdom of Chinese medicine to restore balance or optimal functioning in a group or organization.

Perpetual startup—

a pattern (in individuals or group) of starting but never finishing anything. Examples: a person who has a new idea every week but never brings one to completion, or groups that make "flavor of the month" changes without bringing any of these to evaluation or closure. This leads to wasted resources, a sense of fragmentation and disillusionment.

Step Four—Evaluate Results

If the intervention chosen is in fact what was needed, you will observe a change in the group's energy that allows them to move forward. The intervention may have multiple results or it may have made a subtle difference. If you are successful in doing something to impact energy, it will be evident in the way the group or organization functions. Other interventions may be required at some point, but in many cases the group may be able to take action itself to regain optimal functioning. In the Chinese medicine language this is "trusting the body to heal itself."

If the intervention was not successful, it is necessary to repeat the assessment process and try other interventions. As you work with energy, it is important to move away from the idea of a right way or a wrong way to do things. We need to see this as a process to be entered into with the group or organization—a process that is not right or wrong or good or bad, just a process. Attempts to intervene are much like the role of a midwife who is skilled in knowing how to help along a natural and normal process. Sometimes her intervention involves doing and other times it involves reassessing the situation and waiting quietly and patiently for readiness. Knowing what to do and when to do it comes with time and experience.

Summary

While some aspects of the process outlined in this chapter are similar to other models for intervening in a group process (e.g., assessment, intervention, evaluation), clearly the principles of Chinese medicine offer several unique steps. Very few, if any models used by consultants or organizational development practitioners include the step of noticing and adjusting one's own energy before choosing an intervention. In addition, the Law of Least Action runs counter to the ego-based approach used by some consultants that keeps them in the center of the limelight. This approach is anything but ego driven in that it puts the energy needs of the group as a primary concern. It moves the consultant into a "help around the edges" mode rather than being the center of attention using a "do what I think is best for you" style. This approach requires consultants to recognize their needs to control, impatience with process, or need to be the center of attention. For those who are intrigued by subtlety and nuance, appreciate group process, or love coaching, this model will be a good fit. With time and experience and respect for the wisdom in this model, the steps outlined in this chapter become second nature and effortless.

We turn now to the learning that comes from experience, providing several specific chapters on common individual and organizational challenges. Here we apply the Five Element model to our work with individuals, groups, and organizations. The intent is to demonstrate how these principles apply to concrete, real life situations in a way that conveys the beauty, simplicity, and richness of this ancient wisdom.

Using the
Five Element Model
to Master Change

Jo Manion

Managing change is one of the most profound challenges facing leaders today. The pace of change is accelerating, becoming more complex, and involving fundamental alterations in the way we live, work together, and relate to each other. No one is untouched by change. In organizations across America, people are feeling pressured to "get with the program," to implement change after change, and demonstrate that they are supportive of the organization by willingly adopting the latest "change du jour."

Unfortunately, rather than organizations becoming stronger and our work environments healthier as a result of change, we are seeing exhausted employees, frustrated leaders, and massive amounts of resources being squandered. Yet we now know that change can be accomplished more easily and effectively than the way it is undertaken in most organizations today, whether they are health care or another. The answers can be found by applying the principles of the Five Element model.

Thinking of change as a developmental process and relating it to the Cycle of Development (Shen cycle) offers a tried and true approach to effectively managing change in a system, organization or group, as well as in our personal lives. Change management theories of the past offer insight into how to produce change and recognize various stages of any process. What we need today, however, are more specific techniques for managing, leading, and coping with the rapid and frequent changes we are encountering. Our past experience and education barely prepare us for the swiftness of change today. By its very nature, change is unpredictable and cannot be controlled. However, applying a sequential, logical process to managing and leading change can help us reduce chaos and confusion, and increase our leadership effectiveness.

This chapter explores the application of the Five Element model using each energy as a phase of change (see Figure 10-1). The key functions of the energies are reviewed as they relate to change. A case study and specific examples and applications to health care are provided. Note that the issues of each phase apply whether the change being considered is a large-scale organizational change or changes within the work group or a specific department.

Figure 10-1: The Change Cycle

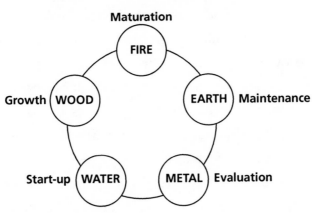

Water Energy—The Startup Phase

In the first phase of a change process (Water Energy), purpose and resource allocation are critical considerations. Initiators of change often are anxious to get started immediately and may lack the patience to complete the work of this phase. However, smoothness of change implementation can be increased by carefully laying necessary groundwork in the early stages. During this first phase—which is related to Water energy and is called startup—the exact purpose of the change is clarified. These basic questions should be asked before starting out:

- Why is this change needed or appropriate at this time?
- Why is it important to patients, customers, employees or the organization?
- How can the organization prepare employees as they undergo or collaborate with implementation of these changes?
- How is this change congruent with the mission of the organization and goals of the department?

It may seem obvious to us, but we often overestimate people's general understanding of the initiative. By clearly defining and articulating the purpose of the initiative, the leader provides a sense of direction for those on whom the change depends for implementation. Clarifying the purpose also focuses people on the change. If, as the leader, you are unable to relate the purpose of the change to something that is meaningful and relevant to those affected, you can expect declining enthusiasm and wavering support as you proceed. For example, to many health care workers, reducing the cost of care still is not as relevant a purpose as are changes to improve quality or increase effectiveness for the patient. You should also consider what this change means to employees personally. What would be of greatest value or interest to them? Be certain that the purpose of the change initiative is not only congruent with, but strongly supportive of, the organization's mission as this increases the likelihood of continued support at all levels.

Resource allocation is the second key consideration related to Water energy. Thorough preparation prior to implementing change requires securing needed resources. Think more broadly about resources and don't limit your assessment only to financial resources. Adequate resources must be made available, including time; availability of coaches, mentors, and other support people in the system; the skills of employees and managers; and interest from employees. What will it cost to implement this change? Are financial resources available? During the implementation, will you need access to people with special skills? Are employees currently dealing with more changes than they can handle? Are people already showing signs of seriously depleted energy? Do employees and managers need to learn additional skills before implementing this new change? Alternatively, do any of these questions really matter? In other words, are you facing potential organizational demise and this change is absolutely required for short- or long-term survival? If so, you may have to take the risk and proceed even in the face of inadequate resources.

Decide whether the resources needed for implementation match up with those you have available. Peter Drucker, the renowned management expert, says that the real work of leadership today is determining how to provide for and stay focused on high priority needs with the scarce resources available. It is tempting to become involved in numerous change initiatives because they all seem desirable, but that doesn't mean you should attempt all of them. Drucker says, "You have to learn to say 'no' when the temptation is to do good. The secret of effectiveness is concentration of the very meager resources you have where you can make a difference."[1]

It is hard to decline an opportunity to change when you strongly believe in the need for it, but an accurate assessment of resources may tell you it may be impossible to carry out. Too many organizational leaders start down a specific path because it seems the thing to do rather than basing their decisions on an actual assessment of resources and the relationship of the change on the organization's mission.

Addressing the issues of this first phase is predominantly a leadership responsibility. But keep in mind that leadership exists at all levels of the organization. Coworkers, employees, and other team members have an active role as well, which is to ask questions about the purpose and direction, to assist in further clarifying it, and to accurately assess current resources affecting their spheres of influence. Once the purpose has been clarified and needed resources identified, it is time to proceed to the next phase—growth and Wood energy. A brief example of an ongoing, successful organizational change illustrates this process in the initial phase.

Case Study

Jane, the CEO of a 320-bed Midwestern hospital, attended a regional health care executive meeting. There she learned about organizational changes in several other facilities involving the implementation of teams and increased responsibility of employees. Throughout her four-year tenure as CEO, her philosophy and practice of highly involving employees had developed momentum in the organization. She clearly recognized the benefits of establishing teams as the basic organizational unit and as a way to build higher levels of employee involvement into the very structure of the organization.

She decided that a way to prepare her organization for an increasingly uncertain future was to accelerate employees' involvement in decision making and problem solving on departmental and organizational issues. For some time, she had been frustrated with a lack of forward movement toward several long-term organizational goals. The level of employee involvement varied widely among departments and depended on each individual manager's philosophy. Work units were poorly structured and did not enhance productivity or effectiveness. It seemed with each passing month the organization was being driven increasingly by a crisis orientation that made it difficult to focus on long-term survival strategies for the system.

Jane was anxious to share these ideas from the conference with her executive colleagues. For this effort to be successful, she would need the full support and involvement of the entire executive leadership group. Although her first inclination was to begin informal discussions, she decided instead to add the topic of teams and employee empowerment to the agenda of the next executive meeting. To prepare, she reflected on how a team-based structure would best fit the mission of the organization. She considered the internal culture and challenges facing the organization in the near future. She also identified problems with the system and areas where performance was unsatisfactory.

One area of major concern for Jane was organizational resources. She considered the following areas—

Financial: Although the hospital was financially sound, lengths of stays had decreased steadily and revenue had significantly dropped during the last few months. Increasing numbers of patients were being covered by managed care contracts, which dictated shorter stays and limited reimbursement. Moreover, the orthopedic surgeons were considering building a free-standing orthopedic hospital.

Management Staff: In recent years, whenever the manager of a small department resigned, another manager was asked to assume the responsibilities of the departing manager rather than hire a replacement. As a result, there had been some minor reductions in managerial staff, but more serious trimming was needed. Management staff tenure averaged twelve years and only a few of the new managers had demonstrated strong, effective leadership skills.

Educational Resource: Internal education efforts had once been impressive, but education department staff had been reduced significantly six years ago during a layoff. Presently, the department provided only mandatory education and training. Because of this limited centralized resource, many departments had developed internal staff to assume responsibilities for education.

Organizational Culture: Employees had been gradually moving from an attitude of entitlement or "you owe me," to an attitude of earning: "I owe you, so that you will owe me." Workers' clinical and technical skills were good and pride in their work was rebounding from a dip after the layoff. Although progress was slow, more employees were beginning to accept responsibility for their behavior and decisions rather than depending on the manager or blaming others when things went wrong. Among staff groups, two seemingly contradictory attitudes prevailed: the first was a "can do" attitude, and the second was a wait and see approach to everything.

Experience with Change: The most significant organization-wide change was the layoff that had occurred two years before Jane's arrival. The layoffs had come as a surprise to employees and several key aspects had been mishandled. Trust and respect for the executive team had been restored during the last four years, but many employees with long memories remained ready to assume the worst. One serious misjudgment made by the decision makers six years ago had been failure to anticipate the emotional reactions of the survivors, the employees who remained. The often publicly expressed attitude of the previous CEO was that employees should be happy they still had jobs!

Timing: The hospital was in the middle of the winter season and a high census was now straining the human resources of the organization. Employees were exhausted from working extra shifts and overtime. This situation was destined to reverse itself within four to six weeks, however, when the hospital would be entering its slower period.

Jane sensed that change would need to begin as soon as possible. The rate of mergers, sales, and closures of regional hospitals and health systems was increasing nationally and she knew the effects would soon be felt in this community. Moving to a team-based structure promised to increase the resiliency, flexibility, and responsiveness to change.

At the executive meeting, Jane introduced the topic of teams by sharing the experiences of colleagues she had met at the regional meeting. The group discussed mutual knowledge and experiences with organizational teams and what they were reading in their professional literature and hearing about when they attended outside meetings. Several executives expressed long-standing interest in the idea. Each agreed individually to explore the concept further. The group scheduled a date and time to revisit the idea.

At the next meeting, the executive team reviewed the mission of the organization and discussed the purpose of a change to becoming more team-based. The actual change was described as "increasing staff's involvement in decision making and problem solving about departmental and organizational issues."

Purposes of the change were identified as follows:

- To improve the delivery of patient care and customer service as a result of better prepared and more involved employees
- To create a flexible, responsive structure enabling the organization to respond quickly to new marketplace forces
- To prepare employees for participation in future organizational changes

Resources needed to support this change included:

- Training (for leaders and employees) with paid time for educational offerings
- Leadership development assistance for current managers
- Increased resources within the education department
- Commitment from the management group
- Support from the board of trustees
- Financial resources to hire external consultants to help develop a group of internal consultants
- Increased time commitment and involvement for leaders at all levels in the organization
- More open communication systems
- Receptivity and trust from employees

Jane and the executive group obtained assistance almost immediately by meeting with and selecting external consultants who were experienced in implementing teams and decentralizing decision making in health care organizations. These consultants were chosen specifically because they were process consultants who would help the organization develop its own solutions and strengthen its internal talent pool. In addition, the executive group began immediately, both individually and with the external experts, to educate themselves as fully as possible. The board of trustees granted the go-ahead for the next phase.

Wood—Growth Phase

In any organization, structural elements needed for supporting change are considered during the second phase, in which Wood energy is predominant. Questions to be asked include:

- What is our vision for the future?
- What structure do we need to bring about this change?
- How will decisions be made about the change and who will make them?
- What kind of committee or task force structure is necessary?
- How will current employee roles and responsibilities be affected throughout the organization?
- What changes will be needed in other organizational systems?

Depending on the nature and scope of the change being considered, a vision for the future is important. A vision is imperative if the change requires people to behave or relate to each other differently—often called a cultural change. Asking people to alter their behavior is usually unsuccessful unless the leader can envision future changes, articulate them clearly, and use this vision to gain commitment from the people who must implement the change. In cases of major change, a clearly articulated vision shared by all is usually the difference between mere compliance and true commitment on the part of employees and leaders alike.

A vision is a critical step for planning to be effective, and planning is a key issue for this phase. If you can see your destination it is easier to determine steps needed to reach it. An implementation plan with assigned responsibilities, specific time frames, and estimated costs is fundamental in organizing and initiating the change. The plan is used to communicate with employees and managers and, in some cases, to obtain needed support from others in the system (e.g., the board, medical staff, and community partners) who can influence the initiative. It also provides a means of measuring progress and alerts you to the need for additional resources that you may have missed in Phase One. Overly rigid plans that cannot be modified or updated hamper creativity because innovative change rarely unfolds as planned.

Case Study

Continuing with the case study, at this point, the executive group worked together to create its vision of the organization for the future. The vision statement read:

Our organization will be a highly responsive and flexible organization within which employees work in an empowered, team-based environment.

The next step was developing a plan the organization could use to arrive at this vision. The executive group established a resource team to serve as in-house experts for both the design and the development of teams. Reporting relationships, boundaries, decision-making parameters and authority between the executive group and the resource team then were established. Finally, selection criteria for resource team appointees and the anticipated time commitment were determined. Executive group members began sharing their vision with other employees. This dialogue reshaped the vision, resulting in stronger commitment house-wide. Although some employees remained skeptical that certain managers could or would behave in ways congruent with this vision, they were generally excited by the possibilities. The new vision statement read:

> *Our organization will be a highly responsive and flexible organization in which employees and leaders work together within an empowered, self-directed, and team-based environment to deliver the highest quality of patient and customer service possible.*

With assistance from the external consultants, the group developed an organization plan that included realistic time frames for each step and clearly assigned responsibilities. Sequencing of departmental implementation was discussed and a preliminary plan approved. The resource team's initial assignment was to establish a process for designing and developing teams. The education department developed an education plan to support these efforts. The executive team worked closely with the resource team and the education department to identify the scope of decision-making responsibility for each. Areas retained by the executive team for their decision making were clearly identified.

Fire—Maturation Phase

Fire energy predominates in the third phase of change management and is referred to as maturation. This is a stage of excitement, enthusiasm, and high energy! The work of the earlier stages is now paying off. Finally there are results, people are working together, and the project seems to have taken on a life of its own. Key issues and functions at this point include coordination and cooperation, determining priorities, internal communications, and the interpersonal aspects of the change.

Close coordination among internal staff, managers, and leaders is critical for any change initiative to work, otherwise employees are left with the impression that "the left hand doesn't know what the right hand is doing." Coordination of the actual implementation plan is a major task. Unfortunately, many examples of poor coordination abound, but one of the most dramatic is the hospital that restructured, redesigned, and opened a major new care center during a predictable peak census period. Just when staff could barely meet service requirements because of volume demand, they also had to learn new processes and work with new team members. The initiative failed and the organization lost months of planning and development time, not to mention credibility with physicians and employees.

When extensive change is occurring, people tend to become more egocentric. Normally cooperative people and departments suddenly seem obstructive and unresponsive.

Anticipate and monitor this reaction to mitigate the negative results. Get cooperation from employees and managers simply by asking for it or stating it as an expectation. You can model cooperation and their expectations for it by openly and frequently sharing information. Better to err on the side of too much information rather than too little.

Staying focused on priorities also helps maintain commitment to the initiative. Reevaluate and restate your priorities as often as needed to communicate continuing support and a sense of urgency for this change. For example, you may be asking people to work in teams and take responsibility for departmental decisions. In the beginning, it seems like decisions take forever to make. If the workload suddenly increases, or a regulatory agency announces a surprise visit, or some other unpredicted and stressful event occurs, resist the urge to revert to the old ways of working. If this change is still a priority, consider adding temporary staff, approving overtime or finding other alternatives during this difficult period. When people know what the priorities are, they remain focused and thus are more efficient. If we revert back to previous practices the minute things become stressful, the message to employees is that this change wasn't really a priority after all.

Communication during change is absolutely essential. Leaders must be able to articulate difficult concepts clearly. If the concept wasn't well understood, be willing to try new approaches, explanations or examples. Key points must be communicated at least seven to eight times before people actually internalize the message. When you are sick to death of discussing this change, you may finally be getting the message through. Frustration over having to repeat yourself is ultimately self-defeating. Expect and receive graciously people's questions even if you feel like you've just finished explaining that answer. If they understood, they wouldn't be asking again.

Sharing the purpose of the change during initial stages of the project is important—but not enough. Identify key stakeholders, those who will be directly affected by the change, and target a communication strategy to each stakeholder group to keep it informed about the implementation process as it progresses.

Sharing information through storytelling is a valuable leadership technique. Stories are powerful motivational tools that not only spread enthusiasm and inspire commitment, they are remembered longer than the facts.[2] Using analogies and metaphors is also powerful in helping people relate this change to things they already know. Remember that people need much more information during change. Uneasiness, anxiety, and fear are predominant emotions of personal transition, and access to clear, current, accurate information is one way to help employees cope with these feelings. Continually sharing examples of successes and experiences of other employees is a way to keep enthusiasm and motivation high.

Remember that formal leaders are not the only sources of communication and information. Encourage employees to create mechanisms to share information with each other. Some departments create a weekly newsletter to keep people updated. Discipline-specific governance structures are also an effective means of communication.

A culture that embodies and values open sharing of information stays healthier and fares better during change. In fact, it may be that more miscommunication results from the manager's attitude than from any particular communication skill.[3] The miscommunications occur as a result of a manager's thoughts, such as, "This is too much information to share," "They can't understand this," "They're not interested in this kind of information," or "It will make their jobs easier if they are told only what they need to know."

Case Study

At this case study hospital, communication and coordination were major concerns of the executive group and resource team. A specific process involving employees had already been developed for communicating with the departments undergoing implementation. Specific communication plans and strategies also had been identified for key stakeholders. The manager and several employees from the involved department became ad hoc members of the resource team for the duration of their department's design and initiation of teams. They handled the communication with the remaining staff.

Meetings were scheduled regularly for employees and departmental leaders. Reactions and ideas were solicited from staff and used to modify the original plans. Although the basic design process didn't change from team to team, by including employees from each department in the design process, the resulting teams accommodated special characteristics unique to the work in each department. Some were skeptical about additional responsibilities delegated to staff and the time it would take for already busy people to assume them. Others doubted whether this change initiative would remain a priority during peak census times. Resource team members and organizational leaders were instrumental in communicating a clear picture of the vision and their personal and collective commitment to it. Before long, several key employees were also sharing the vision with their colleagues.

Teams were designed with the input of employees and based on the needs of patients and families. Rather than have patient-care teams designed by shift or geographical location in the unit, teams instead would be established by patient assignment and geography and would include the entire cadre of direct caregivers assuming responsibilities for the patient. In other words, a team for a small group of patients would include day, evening, night, and weekend shift caregivers. Team membership would remain constant and once a team accepted a patient, it would retain this patient throughout that hospital stay. Teams also were designated by physicians. Most teams were able to provide care consistently for patients of their primary or secondary physicians.

Once teams were designed and members selected, the work of developing as a team ensued. Most employees and leaders showed less understanding of team behavior than they had anticipated. Each team attended educational and training sessions that helped in developing the basic elements of a true team and refreshed communication and problem-solving skills that would be necessary in working together as a team. Many employees were somewhat tentative at first about this change, but as they formed into teams a new sense of momentum developed. As successes occurred, people actually became quite excited about their progress.

Earth—Maintenance Phase

In this phase, the true impact of change is beginning to sink in. Stabilizing the change is an important issue now, otherwise people will revert back to previous behaviors. Methods of anchoring this change in the current reality of the organization or department include formalizing structures or processes that were used during a trial period, establishing new routines, or formally communicating the new processes to key stakeholders. An example of anchoring is to include time for a report about this change at regular employee or management meetings.

Another powerful and effective method of firmly anchoring a change is to modify the reward system of the organization to ensure that new behaviors are continued. Reward systems here refer to both the formal reward or compensation system as well as less formal recognition efforts. Recognizing employee and leadership groups for their contributions to the change effort can take the form of monetary bonuses or small gifts. Just as powerful are opportunities for external recognition and applause. For example, the manager can pay expenses and provide time for participants to attend and/or speak at national and regional meetings. Interviews and articles in both the organization's and the employee's discipline-specific journals are also positive. The key principle is to reinforce the behaviors you want to continue and stop reinforcing those you wish to replace.

Productivity is a second key issue of Earth energy, with several implications for leaders. Remember that when things first change, it takes longer to accomplish the same results. Recall the last time you purchased a new word processing program or received an update to your old system—it took longer initially to generate the same work you could do quickly in the old program. Many decisions to change are based on an expectation of improved productivity; however, this improvement almost never occurs at the beginning of any change initiative. Expect productivity to drop initially (in direct proportion to the size of the change) and improvements to come later. Be certain that expected time frames for achieving this improvement are appropriate and be realistic, because you may be held to those improvements you promised. It is better to under-promise and over-deliver than vice versa.

Closely related to productivity is the critical need for people in the organization to take good care of themselves. Change can be exhilarating, frightening, and dangerously exhausting. If leaders and employees don't replenish their energy on a regular basis, the change initiative may cost the organization some of its best people. The yang energies, Wood and Fire, exemplify expenditure. Earth energy is the transition element as the cycle moves from yang to yin energy. At this phase, the work turns toward replenishment. Employees and leaders alike can sustain the highest level of productivity and personal effectiveness only if they take opportunities for self-renewal. And, if this behavior isn't modeled by leaders in the organization, it doesn't matter what you say about the need for employees to take care of themselves. They observe the frenetic, workaholic behavior of their leaders and conclude that this out-of-balance behavior is what is really expected and rewarded in the system.

Case Study

As change was implemented in the case study during the first several months, the productivity in the restructured departments decreased. A great deal of time was spent in meetings and things just took longer to accomplish. But Jane and the executive group had anticipated this and had negotiated new financial performance parameters with the board. They agreed on a critical process point at which they would reevaluate this agreement.

Managers and leaders had often found that it was easier just to do a job themselves. The entire leadership group had to remind each other continually of the commitment to transfer real responsibility to the teams. The support between the executive group and resource team members had helped in reaffirming their commitments during the early stages of the change. Employees were encouraged to remain balanced and to take good care of themselves. Executives also modeled this behavior as best they could. Moreover, teams were given permission to be flexible in providing required coverage for their clinical or technical work and in performing teamwork (i.e., problem-solving meetings, coordination efforts, etc.).

Members of the executive group and resource team continually provided positive reinforcement when they observed behaviors that supported the new vision. Articles were published frequently in the organization's newsletter to highlight and emphasize results. They reinforced any positive movement that showed employee teams accepting more responsibility for issues and problems within their working groups. When behaviors contradicted the original purpose, redirection was provided. One team, for example, was experiencing some interpersonal difficulties and brought the problem to one of the managers. The manager did not take responsibility for solving the problem but, instead, coached the team in ways they could deal with the behaviors.

Metal—Evaluation Phase

Evaluation or closure is the final phase of this developmental cycle for managing change and includes evaluation of the process, results, and quality of the project. Often overlooked or undervalued, this phase is critical for both the current and future change initiatives in the organization. Is the change successful? How do you know? Did you obtain the results you desired and projected? Can you evaluate the effectiveness of this project? What is the impact on organizational quality of service? Has quality demonstrably improved? What indicators prove this?

Besides answering these questions, the actual implementation process should be evaluated at this time. What were the lessons learned during the implementation? What would you do differently next time? What did you and the employees learn about resiliency in dealing with change? What were the emotional reactions? What did and did not work? Sharing these lessons openly—the successes as well as the mistakes—in the organization is an effective way of creating and increasing organizational learning.

Closure, or letting go, is another aspect of this phase as well as a critical leadership function. Effective closure is the beginning stage of transition and positions people well for the next change. Yet closure is perhaps the least understood and most often overlooked issue of the entire developmental cycle. Putting formal closure on the change project is a goal in dealing with this phase. Celebration ceremonies at this stage can be effective—whether simple or elaborate. The key is to link celebrations to specific performance whenever possible. If a team just successfully completed a phase of a project or enjoyed a significant success, order the pizza today! Waiting until next week or later in the month takes the spontaneity and fun out of the reward. Ensure that there has been a true accomplishment and that the celebration is not just recognition of existence!

However, completing a project also includes the emotion of grief as core groups are disbanded or a leader's responsibilities are changed. The need for grieving cannot be underestimated during this phase. Effective leaders will assist staff in expressing and dealing constructively with these feelings so that the individuals involved will be ready for the next project. Bill Bridges' work on managing transitions is a helpful model to use in dealing with the emotional issues of closure. See *Managing Transitions: Making the Most of Change.*[4]

Case Study

The evaluation of the project in this case study was exciting. Before-and-after measurement indicators, such as physician and patient/customer satisfaction levels, showed improvements in both areas. Productivity figures varied from department to department. In areas where employees were already functioning well at independent and interdependent levels, productivity decreased only slightly and rebounded and improved more rapidly than anticipated. Yet in departments where employees depended heavily on the manager for decision making prior to the change, productivity figures were disappointing, even months after implementation. As part of their evaluation, each team's developmental level was measured. Almost all teams in the organization showed progress in their stages of development.

The resource team also initiated an evaluation process that followed each department's implementation and identified lessons learned. Many of these were used to improve future implementations, and involved the way employees handled change and what methods were and were not effective. For example, teams discovered the need to organize cross-team task forces to deal with issues that affected everyone in the department. They also discovered the need for more training on facilitation skills to support effective team problem solving. The evaluation process also provided a tracking system for measuring the transfer to the teams of traditional management functions, such as financial monitoring and budgeting, planning, and performance appraisals. These responsibilities were scheduled to be transferred to the teams over a gradual time period.

Rather than waiting until the entire project was completed, each department planned a celebration at the end of its implementation. Because of the nature of work shifts, it was difficult to have an event that all employees could attend together. So, two activities were planned. The first was a potluck open house for all shifts, with team members providing the food. Physicians or other customers (internal and external) often were invited by the team. Second, each team planned its own celebration when it reached its six-month anniversary as a team and was meeting its outcome measures. Besides these activities, each department installed a bulletin board in a prominent place highlighting the membership and accomplishments of its teams for customers and other hospital employees to see.

The Five Element Model: A Developmental Process for Managing Change

Using the Five Element model is useful for both small- and large-scale initiatives. Each group goes through the same sequence in beginning its work as a team. The basic principles and issues of each phase provide a check-point to measure progress.

Although changes may actually start in any one of these phases, they progress more smoothly if these phases are followed sequentially. No change will realize its full potential unless the issues of each energy as outlined here are addressed and managed. If any of the key issues are glossed over or inadequately dealt with, problems occur. Examples of failed change efforts abound. How many times have we done a great job with the first three phases—people are excited and working together well to get results—but nothing is put in place to stabilize the change? Then, when the manager or a key leader leaves, within weeks everyone has reverted to the old way of doing things. Or the project is "dead in the water" because there are no resources dedicated to support it. Or an overly enthusiastic leader initiated too many changes at once and, because employees lacked the energy to implement all of them, failed to do any very well.

How many times do we implement change yet fail to follow up to see whether it has made a significant difference in the quality of service or in the value we provide our customers? How many changes fail because we didn't take the time to completely evaluate an earlier project and so we repeat the same mistakes? These are examples of failures resulting partly because the major concerns of each energy were not addressed and managed.

Summary

The Cycle of Development (Shen cycle) is clearly one of the most useful ways to understand change. Change means to alter or to modify...the very nature of generation is to create something new. Applying the Five Element model for guiding change reduces the energy required to make change. It also increases the likelihood of successful change that people in the organization can support.

The Five Energies and the Challenge of a New Position

Jennifer Jenkins

We know that absence of change is death. Even at rest, living organisms are undergoing small, homeostatic changes to preserve balance, equilibrium, and renewal. Change for many people is energizing. For others it is energy depleting. What makes some people welcome and seek change and others avoid it? Changing one's job or position affects not only the person changing but those around him or her as well. Can that change become so overwhelming that it threatens the health and well-being of the individual, the organization? How should the energy of change be managed so that the best outcome can be achieved for everyone?

At the individual level, application of the Shen cycle is ideal for understanding the life cycle of a job. It is also useful for pinpointing strategies that assist during this transformation in the professional arena of life.

Changing jobs or positions can threaten personal and professional balance. Different values, priorities, systems, communication paths, and directions can conflict with personal choices. Learning new tasks and roles affect your ability to organize time and to sequence activities effectively. If the new position is a self-employment opportunity, cash flow problems can affect the ability to grow the business. For those re-entering the workforce after working for themselves, it means losing some flexibility and personal choice in return for the security of more stable compensation and/or benefits.

People who have made the transition successfully from one job to another offer this advice.

- Have a clear purpose and sound goals.
- Utilize effective planning and decision making.
- Negotiate roles, responsibilities, expectations, and schedules (with coworkers, family, and significant others).
- Set priorities, sort activities, manage time, and focus your efforts.
- Keep a healthy sense of humor.
- Use comfortable routines and systems.
- Periodically evaluate your personal and professional life and "clean house."
- Choose to work and live with others who have congruent (not necessarily the same) values,

purposes, approaches, and methods.

- Challenge yourself daily to try new things and expose yourself to new ideas.

This looks like an intimidating list of things to remember. The Five Element model is an effective organizational tool to help you. When blended with findings and knowledge from western schools of management, the model helps us put what we have to do in a framework for change.

Before we revisit the model, let us review a few important points. First, our western culture tends to emphasize activity over reflection. Second, our organizations often fail to understand the impact of the organization on the individual and vice versa. And finally, most organizations are not balanced in their energy. This results in too much emphasis on some energies (over-achievement) and too little emphasis in other energies (under-achievement).

Changing positions and jobs brings an opportunity for fresh approaches, new directions, and exposure to other systems and values. This is true both for the individual involved in the change and the organizations and groups that he or she leaves and enters. By leaving a position, the individual opens it up for someone else to inject refreshing new directions. And by entering a new position, the group is exposed to fresh approaches and ideas. The key is not to expect the new person to be the same as the predecessor, but expect the new person to challenge the status quo by evaluation of what is best to keep and what may be best to discard.

Interrelatedness of Organizations and Individuals

How many of us have been in organizations where a particular position never stays filled very long? For any number of reasons, it is the one often labeled as a "tough position to fill." During exit interviews people who have held this position express frustration with not being able to get the right resources, having ongoing problems with the supervisor or admitting that the "job is impossible."

Supervisors say that they "just can't find good help" for a position, or that people "just don't want to do a good job." Frequent absenteeism and real or perceived illnesses and injuries are symptomatic of dissonance between the organization and the individual position.

If you go for an interview and find that the position you are applying for has had several people in it within the last year or two, be concerned that there may be something about the position that makes it unlikely for incumbents to succeed. And, if you find yourself in a position in which you are uncharacteristically unsuccessful, it may be the position and not you.

Organizations usually reflect the biases of their leaders. When evaluating a new position or a new organization, try to determine what is important to the leaders. Jobs and positions that support those values will likely be better supported with resources, time, and encouragement. Positions that may be necessary to the organization's success, but not interesting to the leaders, will likely receive minimum resources and support.

The Five Element Model Applied to Taking a New Position

The beauty of using the Five Element model is that it follows nature's change cycles and reflects healthy business practices. It is intuitive for most people and expands upon that intuition. Remember that energy generally moves in a clockwise direction. An element feeds the one following it and drains energy from the preceding element. Each element also controls excesses in another (e.g., Wood controls Earth, Water controls Fire).

Water Energy

Water is the element of generation, beginning cycles and starting anew. It is characterized by reflection and moves us to action. We assess our resources, allocate them, and decide on a new direction or mission (or job/position). When you first look for a new job, you may find that you don't know where to start. To help yourself, decide upon a specific goal and make a list of your strengths and the types of positions you enjoy, or think you would enjoy. Then search the job market for the right positions to help you meet that goal. You may make many lists—revising, adding, and deleting before you feel comfortable with your decision.

If you are a person uncomfortable in Water energy, you may find the ambiguity of finding a new position uncomfortable and be tempted to rush through the process to complete this phase. You may not seek or accept a position where the level of ambiguity is high. Individuals who are confident in their own resources are more likely to feel comfortable in Water energy.

They are also more likely to prefer roles that offer a variety of opportunities, wish to personalize responsibilities within the role, and seek flexibility to redesign the job as it unfolds. They are comfortable with ambiguity.

Once you accept a position, you will undoubtedly experience a period of time before you actually begin working. Water types in general are thrilled at the opportunity to explore in their minds how a new job offers them opportunities to grow and learn new skills. They use the waiting time to allow their anticipation to grow and their resources to mobilize. They start the new job with an explosion of activity and enthusiasm.

If this energy is less natural or more uncomfortable for you, this waiting period may be one of growing anxiety and fear. Questions enter your mind: Is this the right job? What if I don't like it? What if I can't do this? What if they don't think I am right for the job? Will I have wasted my time and money? Left unchecked, this anxiety may cause you to grow disenchanted by the time you begin working and you may find it difficult to mobilize the necessary energy to do a good job.

In any new job, most people experience occasional periods of anxiety, doubt, and confusion. As the new job unfolds, unanticipated changes and nuances arise that can be unsettling. This is not unlike being dropped into the middle of the ocean with no idea how deep it is or how far to shore. Expect to question your decision in taking the new position: Can I find the right combination to make this work? Does my boss see the value of what I am doing? How will I learn everything? All these questions have an element of fear in them—the emotion of Water energy. What you do with this emotion determines how well you move to the next energy phase.

To progress, you must mobilize your resources: take stock of why you took the position, your strengths, the new opportunities ahead, and the possibilities of exerting change on the new system you are in. When you do this, you can move out of fear and into Wood energy.

As you begin your new job, keep in mind that others around you are also experiencing change, a period of ambiguity, and feelings of anxiety or fear. Some of this is because your style and behaviors are different than the person who previously held the position. This change adds a new dynamic to relationships and also impacts how the organization moves forward. It is important to consider how to handle this aspect of the change. Actions taken have a great influence on the team effort and motivation. These also impact the overall health and the forward momentum of the organization in general.

Wood Energy

Solidifying your position requires creating a vision, putting actual plans into place, and transforming your ideas and resources into workable activities and outcomes. Missing any of these elements can limit success. In a new job, vision must precede planning and idea generating must be followed by action.

A gardening analogy can illustrate the need to respect this sequence and the completeness of this approach. Many people find it pleasant to plant a garden and watch the seeds sprout. Gardening also requires attention to process. Some aspects of this we might enjoy and others we might find tedious or tend to overlook. We can be completely absorbed on a nice spring day in our garden and then suddenly discover that hours have passed. Consider a garden that is well-planned, where the early growth is fostered and nutrients are added according to a timetable. Imagine how different the garden would be if there were no plan, or if timetables for nutrients were arbitrary or overlooked entirely.

The energy of Wood is focused. The planning can be as absorbing as the process of carrying out the plan. You may work long hours at your new job and not even realize the amount of time you are contributing. You flesh out your early plans and begin to make decisions that affect how, why, when, and by whom work is done. And this is when you are likely to experience the emotion of Wood that is anger.

Until you actually exert change on others in the organization, you are likely to meet with little outward resistance. But change someone's responsibilities, or ask them to stop doing something they have done for years, and watch the fireworks. They may actively resist you or passively work around you. Either way, you and they experience periods of frustration and anger. In addition, your family and significant others may react angrily if you are not with them as much as before the new job. You may feel anger or experience a sense of betrayal when you find the job is not what was portrayed to you when you interviewed. On all fronts, you can expect at least some degree of anger.

Flexibility is key. Just as a young tree is flexible in the wind and does not break like the old, dry, aged trees, you must maintain your flexibility to be successful in the Wood energy phase. Consider obstacles as opportunities. Examine your options, get other opinions, listen to colleagues and coworkers. Use what you learn to review and creatively revise your plans to find even better ways of reaching your goals. Pick and choose your battles. Fight on principle, but give and take on process. The old adage is true—there is more than one way to reach any goal.

Fire Energy

Flexibility helps mobilize energy in you and those around you. As you move into Fire energy, you find your new position influences an even greater number of people and activities in the organization. The Fire element functions are to develop synergy through negotiation, networking, marketing (internal and external), coordination, sorting, prioritizing, and, finally, effective problem solving. Humor and laughter are essential components of Fire energy. Using them frequently drains off the anger and frustration you may have felt in the growth (Wood) phase of your new job. At this phase in the transition to your new position, things explode. This is the time when you feel capable and you are finally seeing results. All the work you did in the Water and Wood phases has paid off. Things are coming together.

Open communication keeps everyone informed and less resentful. Negotiating for win-win solutions, whenever feasible, permits the energy of the whole group to mobilize behind projects. Teamwork builds synergy. It is Fire energy that clearly demonstrates that more is achieved working together than by each person working alone. Individuals who recognize and use this energy can ignite a spark of excitement and enthusiasm into a maelstrom of excitement and a feeling of mastery. By ensuring that people inside and outside the organization/group know and understand the mission, plans, resources, and decisions, success as seen in Fire energy is enhanced.

Knowing how to work within Fire energy and when to move on is one of the most critical organizational challenges in western businesses. This energy is charismatic and infectious. With its associated laughter and humor, it feels warm and desirable. However, like everything else, too much of a good thing can spoil everything,

When you have used your new position to make change in the organization, know when to control the Fire and find ways to continue activities without the same high-energy expenditure. Without doing this, you and/or the organization burn out prematurely. Find time for your family and friends.

When you feel the need to begin looking for ways to standardize some activities, increase productivity, and recognize the contribution of those around you, you are moving into Earth energy...

Earth Energy

One day you realize that you are no longer struggling so hard to get things done. Your coworkers know their roles in the system and work together with you in relative harmony. You are even finding time to start reflecting on what you have achieved. There is a rhythm to your job and you find that much work can be accomplished with minimal effort and thought.

Occasional nagging, often conflicting thoughts intrude: Is this just easy, or have I forgotten something? Isn't it great that everyone is working so well together? Perhaps I am not needed as much? I am not bored, but shouldn't this be harder? Customers are happy, but I wonder if we are doing all we can do? Perhaps I should take that long vacation to Alaska that we've talked about for so long.

This period of comfortable activity is not unlike the end of summer when everything slows down. Gardens and yards don't grow as fast. Fruits ripen, grow heavy and fall. The air is thick, often warm and humid. Most of us would just as soon sip lemonade in the shade rather than work long hours in the sun. We look for ways to get work done without extra exertion. And we begin to look forward to the contraction of daylight, the crispness of the air, and the general cleaning out of old gardens, leaves, and summer places.

In any job held over a long-term period, there is also a time of slowing and ease. Your work becomes easier and more routine. You have more time to reflect and spend with friends and family. Processes are so routine that they can be accomplished by many different people, making the organization more flexible. You may be surprised at how balanced you feel. Time and resources are managed effortlessly. Clients and coworkers are comfortable with you and you can empathize with their concerns. However, you are clear about what their responsibility is in resolving those concerns and what is yours.

This process of slowing down and feeling the rhythms of life around you is the essence of Earth energy. It prepares you for the even slower and more reflective energy of Metal. Failure to move out of this comfortable energy, however, results in stagnation. Just as a good "cold snap" startles us into autumn, so must we recognize that slowing is not dying, but preparation for the hard work of evaluation and distillation.

Metal Energy

Every position reaches a point where it must be evaluated for continuance, modification or deletion. It is important in all businesses, but especially in our action-oriented western ones, that we take time to figure out if our jobs are important and necessary. With Earth energy slowing us down, we now have time to reflect on how well we have done in our new job. To be truly effective, our evaluation should be built into each evolutionary phase of a position: at the end of probation, at key decision points in a project, at the end of a project, and certainly at least once a year.

In Metal energy we find the need to reduce our job to its component parts and contributions. Is this the job you set out to do? Has it evolved to meet your needs or just the needs of the organization? What aspects of the job do you enjoy? What have you learned? Is this job going to be useful in new projects within the organization? Where do you go next? What will you do? If you stay and the job remains, what do you need in the way of resources to move forward? What new directions does the job need to take and do you want to go the same way?

It is likely that you feel a mixture of sadness and happiness as this phase in your professional life comes to a close. As you celebrate the joys of successes you have achieved, recognize there is also a degree of anxiety and excitement about new opportunities. If you are leaving the organization, you may feel a sense of personal and professional loss. On the other hand, if the experiences have not been positive, it is possible that this is reflected in relief and excitement about new adventures.

By evaluating and reflecting on what has been learned, what is most valuable, and what you want to take with you into new positions, you gain inspiration and energy to propel you into yet another cycle. If you are unable or unwilling to do this, you may find yourself stuck in a job you do not like, and cannot or will not do well in. You also will likely not be a part of any new directions taken by the organization. Eventually you will become hardened and brittle, like old metal. So keep moving, taking the best you have gained, and plunge ahead into your next opportunity—whether a new job or a reinvention of the one you have.

Lessons Learned

Using the Five Element model to manage your own energy as you take a new position can help you increase your chances for success. The following chart gives you some concrete activities for each stage to ensure that you stay balanced and healthy.

Table 11-1: Energy Interventions

Element: Water (Clear purpose/goals; adequate resources)

Actions:
- Put your purpose/goals on paper.
- Post them where you see them every morning.
- Review your resources to do your job well (time, cash flow, reserves, skills, support systems, people, space, etc.).
- Know how to access additional resources if needed.
- If you experience thirst, back pain, kidney or bladder problems, pay attention—you may be experiencing imbalance in this energy.

Element: Wood (Planning and decision making)

Actions:
- Develop workable action plans.
- Include realistic timelines.
- Assign tasks to those who are able to complete them; support them.
- Be sure your job description and those of others reflect the realities of your jobs.
- Listen and incorporate others' ideas into the plan.
- Make decisions in a timely manner.
- If you make a mistake, fix it and move on.
- Pay attention to headaches, tautness and rigidity, eye strain, muscle cramps, anger—they may be evidence of imbalance in this energy.

Element: Fire (Priorities, sorting, coordination, communication, public relations)

Actions:
- Set priorities to focus your energy on important activities.
- Coordinate activities to minimize wait times and redundant work.

- Communicate in a variety of ways to ensure that everyone hears your message.

- Work on developing healthy relationships.

- Work to create an environment for success both internally and externally.

- Keep a sense of humor; laugh.

- Pay attention to feelings of dryness, insomnia, heart racing or skipping, high blood pressure, inability to sit still, fatigue—these may indicate an imbalance in this energy.

Element: Earth (Routines, systems, recognition, and support)

Actions:
- Streamline processes, utilize the advantages of information systems, tickler files, or excellent office managers to improve efficiency and effectiveness.

- Find ways of recognizing achievements (yours and others).

- Pay attention to sudden changes in weight, excessive feelings of sympathy and worry, muscle weakness, strong sweet tooth or apathy—these may indicate imbalance in this energy.

Element: Metal (Evaluation, quality control, inspiration)

Actions:
- Evaluate your performance and those of your coworkers critically and objectively.

- Eliminate work, ideas, or job categories that are no longer helpful to the mission and purpose (yours or the organization).

- Identify key ideas, processes, skills, knowledge, etc., that are important to carry forward.

- Arrange these in a new "story"—that is, a way of describing them to others so that they can understand and be inspired to achieve them.

- Pay attention to exacerbation of allergies or asthma, excessive or deficient grief, over-attention to details, need for hierarchy, a sense of isolation, bowel disturbances—these may indicate imbalance in this energy.

- Capture the excitement of new opportunities and move on to a new job or a renewal of your existing one.

Summary

Remember, your new job or position can enhance or detract from your health. All five elements become important as you search and move into a new job or position. Remaining in any one energy for extended periods can lead to imbalance and to stagnation. Differences of opinion, style, and process all are vital to the continuing evolution of our systems. Therefore, as you take on your new opportunity, seek out those who disagree with you as much as those who agree. The diversity of the two will enrich you and keep you vital.

In health there is a dynamic balance that self-corrects and energizes us personally and professionally. In any job, there is time for both the energy expenditures required of the yang energy, the Wood and Fire elements, and the renewal side, Earth, Metal, and Water. Both sides are necessary. When one or the other is out of balance, adjusting the energy flow can ensure health. Life is change. Let your new job or position be life.

12

The Five Energies and Contemporary Organizational Challenges

Sharon Cox and Jo Manion

In previous chapters we described the symmetry, simplicity, and insight inherent in the Five Element model. At this point you may well be asking, "How does this relate to my life?" Indeed, how does this ancient wisdom relate to the challenges we all face in today's organizations?

This chapter makes the connection. By reviewing the key functions of each of the Five Elements and relating them to current issues in health care, we are able to see the relevance of this model to organizational life right now. This chapter explores each element using examples of actual issues from a variety of organizations.

Water Energy—
Service Excellence, A Compelling Mission

The Water element is perfectly expressed by the Ford Motor Company, which uses the motto: "At Ford, quality is job one." But we in the health care arena know that a clear sense of mission permeating the work culture has not been the norm. In health care the picture could more aptly be captured with the phrase, "We are all things to all people." This lack of clarity has not served us well in staying focused on getting results. On a positive note, in the last four or five years we have seen a number of organizations that have chosen to correct this long-standing issue with a clear, organization-wide effort around what is commonly called a culture of service excellence. This effort to move from scattered priorities and multiple goal statements to one over-arching theme of service excellence provides a vivid example of the power of Water energy to motivate an entire organization.

In organizations taking this approach, the work to be done is typically focused around several identified key dimensions: Service, Quality, Finances, and Growth. These are the pillars because they are foundational and serve as a basis for decision making.[1] A senior executive in Florida who helped to implement a common approach using these pillars comments:

> We used to have pages and pages of strategic goals and
> initiatives and it was hard to keep up with what was actually

getting accomplished. As we focused on these "pillars," we worked through the pages of goals and decided if the goal did not fit under one of these foundational pillars, then the organization was choosing to omit it. It was the first time in my thirty years in health care that I had ever seen us take anything off our list of goals. I knew in that meeting that we were serious about changing the culture and that this was not just a "flavor of the month" effort like we had had so many times in the past. My trust is this culture change effort was much greater after I watched the executive team make those hard choices.[2]

As executive teams get serious about a clear sense of mission, they often find that this shift from multiple priorities to a limited number of foundational themes requires their whole-hearted support and constant reinforcement. In this hospital, the senior team and middle managers routinely make rounds to determine how change efforts are going and to identify system problems that need their attention. The Human Resources Department puts out a weekly memo, called "Pillar Talk," to be used by managers in reinforcing a key theme of customer service. These weekly reminders were helpful to employees as they worked on integrating principles of customer service into their routine practice. Customer service scores are tabulated weekly and discussed monthly in management meetings as further evidence that the organization is making every effort to be congruent with their value of customer service.[3]

A culture of service excellence often gets good employee buy-in because the effort to improve customer service is predicated on the notion that only "satisfied employees can deliver high-quality customer service."[4] For this reason, a concerted effort to have employees feel valued is ongoing, with regular thank-you notes from their managers and rounding by managers and senior executives, who ask the question: "What can I do to make you more successful?" This focus on employee satisfaction as a means to improve patient satisfaction has proven to be successful. Some organizations experience significant improvements in patient satisfaction scores and market share after just one year of operating with a clear intention of customer service.

However, Water energy is not only about mission but also about resources, and this increase in market share has often resulted in organizations having a much healthier financial picture in a relatively short time. The six-hundred-bed hospital referenced earlier went from a negative bottom line to making over $10 million annually in a four-year span. While not all efforts to get focused as an organization yield such results, it is obvious that the clearer sense of mission and purpose can also lead to a better use of resources as each department becomes intentional about improving customer service.[5]

Another way this impacts the effective use of resources relates to employee turnover. This executive found that the highly visible effort to change the culture and to focus on a central theme of customer service even had a positive impact on employee turnover.

"We have probably lost about sixty or seventy employees during the last four years that we needed to lose because they really did not fit in this culture and they self-selected out...

(The self-selection process) was not anything that the managers did specifically to deal with certain people who were not on board with customer service; it just seemed as if it dawned on them that there wasn't going to be a thank-you note coming to their home and so they moved on to places that were a better fit for them."[6]

Another example of the power of a clear mission and attention to needed resources can be seen in the employee selection process as well. A manager in the coronary care unit related his experience when the employees with whom he worked turned down a prospective candidate who he thought was very qualified. When he asked the employees for their reasoning they were very articulate in giving their rationale.

"We talked with her for over an hour and she commented several times on how much she loved troubleshooting equipment problems in the ICU, and that she saw her technical skills as her best talent. Each time we brought up a discussion of customer service as our theme in this unit she seemed to discount that. It was clear to us the more we listened that she loved to nurse the machines and not the patients so we all agreed that she would not be a good fit for this unit."[7]

In another department, a group of employees who were committed to a healthy work climate and maintaining their good customer satisfaction scores even chose to send one of their coworkers home when she repeatedly began coming to work with a negative attitude. They explained to the manager the next day that they had tried several other interventions, to no avail, so they simply redid the day's assignment, with each of them taking one of her patients. The employee with the negative attitude was asked to go home until she could do something about her attitude.[8]

In both of these examples of employee actions, the employees trusted that they had their managers' support and were all in agreement about the primacy of customer service in their work environment. Employees taking ownership for good use of resources is clear evidence that the culture in the organization can change. In fact, when attention is given to developing a clear sense of mission and purpose as well as the proper use of resources, powerful change can occur in a short period of time.

Wood Energy—Implementing Shared Decision-making Models

One of the positive aspects of the current workforce shortages in health care has been that health care facilities have begun to ask the question: How do we create a culture for retention by improving working conditions for employees? As they consider what changes they need to make to create a more positive work environment they are often grappling with a vision of how to improve the climate for professional practice or the plan for implementing or enhancing a shared governance structure or a shared decision-making model.[9] In other words, they are grappling with the various dimensions of Wood energy.

Changes in nursing practice are a good example of this. The visioning process used to transform the nursing work environment for many organizations has been aided by using

226

an evidence-based model developed by the American Nurses Credentialing Center. Through a nationwide credentialing process involving rigorous standards, the ANCC recognizes hospitals that provide excellent nursing services and foster a work climate that attracts nurses. Referred to as Magnet Certification, this credentialing process was initially seen as having marketing potential or as a public relations advantage in a competitive market. Over time the standards on which the certification process is based can clearly provide a vision and a structure for making significant changes in the health care workplace. In the *Journal of Nursing Administration*, Stolzenberger writes about using the Magnet Recognition framework: "The real promise lies in its potential to transform the practice climate in ways that empower nurses, advance professional practice, and improve patient outcomes."[10]

This attention to workplace culture and to best practices has led some organizations to not only involve nurses more in decision making about their work environment, but to expand their decision-making process to include those in other professional disciplines as well. Recognizing the need to move away from the hierarchical, top-down decision making that has characterized hospitals for more than one hundred years, a number of hospitals and health care organizations have begun to rethink their structure for decision making to make it more inclusive. This effort to move decision making down in the organization is often referred to as "shared governance" (typically in nursing departments) or "shared accountability" or "shared decision making," as decision-making councils involve all professional disciplines and not just nursing.[11]

Shared governance—

the process and structure by which decision making is decentralized in an organization so that decisions are made closest to the situation or issue.

A Michigan medical center elected to change its process for decision making as its leaders envisioned ways they could create a culture for retention. As part of their vision for culture change they opted to form a design team made up of department directors and a few representatives from the executive team charged with developing a plan for implementing a shared decision-making model.[12] This design team was a microcosm of Wood energy as they put together a flow chart with time frames and key decision-making points, and as they grappled in weekly meetings with different views on how to best complete their task. The vice president for Organizational Development, who chaired this design team, relates the struggles they had in working through conflictual issues and reaching consensus.

> We spent several meetings reviewing data collected by subgroups and then working on a structure that would incorporate the group's best thinking. We set ground rules as to how we would deal with each other and found that over time we were able to talk out our differences and reach consensus, which we defined as 70 percent agreement and 100 percent support. This was not an easy or rapid process and in fact took almost one year to implement the structure we designed.[13]

The councils identified in this model make decisions around the categories of Strategy, People and Culture, Patient Care, and Operations. An integration team made up of the chairpersons of these four councils coordinates the activities of the councils and acts as an oversight group. Recently, as the organization struggled with a financial downturn, the executive team turned to directors involved in Operations for their best thinking about where and how to cut expenses. Several of the suggestions made by this group were implemented and this added credence to their sense that the days of top-down decision making were over.[14]

In listening to this design team reflect on their lessons learned in the process of creating this very different approach to decision making, there were often references to the essential nature of Wood energy. They referred to how helpful it was to display their thinking on flip charts and use flow charts to track their progress in a visual way. They laughed about how they struggled initially with their differences and had to take some time to get to know each other before they could work well together.

They also related the anxiety they felt as they reached key decision-making points and had to make their case in presentations to the executive team. "We have struggled with the real meaning of shared decision making and had to recognize that it is not just putting councils together, but rather a new way of relating to each other in a collaborative way, as partners in a process—and this has been a huge change," this vice president commented as she reflected on the work of the design team in concert with the executive team. "This has been a lengthy and sometimes arduous process as we worked out council charters and details about what the structure needed to look like, but in the long run we know our decisions will be better and that makes it worth all the effort."[15]

While developing a vision or implementing a new structure are classic examples of ways in which Wood energy is evidenced in the work environment, another common organizational issue related to Wood energy involves the structure for meetings. What kind of meetings do we need? How often should these groups get together? Who should attend? How do we reach consensus on an issue? Working on the structure and timing for meetings as well as the infrastructure for the decision-making process naturally brings up conflict, the essential emotion in Wood energy. Lencioni, in his best-selling book, *The Five Dysfunctions of a Team*, cautions that until a group learns to manage its differences, rather than resorting to artificial harmony or meetings after the meeting, the goal of becoming a cohesive team is unlikely.[16] Productive meetings are a prerequisite for teamwork, and using Wood energy appropriately can make all the difference.

Fire Energy—
Creating Community, Teams, Innovation

One of the best indicators of healthy Fire energy in an organization is a pervasive sense of teamwork and esprit de corps with a keen sense of commitment, not just to one's own unit or department, but to the organization as a whole. A Colorado hospital offers a prime example of this aspect of Fire energy. I (Sharon) had been invited there a few years ago to provide a seminar for nurses as part of a week-long celebration of Nurses Week. While on a break after the morning seminar I had the opportunity to walk through the building and have lunch. I noticed employees in the cafeteria who were laughing and joking with colleagues (physicians and nurses, respiratory techs, and lab staff) and obviously enjoying their time there. I visited with a family friend and listened to her talk about her wonderful team of nurses and how they felt like part of her family. I could sense a camaraderie and warmth among the nurses in the staffing office as I watched them work together to problem solve staffing issues for the afternoon shift.

Later that day as I finished the second seminar I commented to the nurses gathered there that I could feel a difference in their facility that was so noticeable it made me want to sign up to work there. One of them said to me on the way out that day, "That difference you picked up on is for real, we all know it, and that is why we are here." A year later this hospital was designated a Magnet Hospital, having met the rigorous standards for excellence established by the American Nurses Credentialing Center. They have established the kind of work environment that health care professionals are drawn to and clearly that "magnet" status is for real.

The sense of connection and teamwork so reflective of healthy Fire energy was also evident at a Washington medical center as a group of staff members working with geriatric patients were brought together for an annual goal-setting session. The group was asked as part of their reflection on the accomplishments of the last year to think of a time when they had experienced the "essence of teamwork" and the impact this had on them. With a group of fifty people gathered there, they began to tell stories of how their fellow nurses had supported them through family crises, illness, and the loss of long-term patients. There was not a dry eye in the group as they shared their stories. One of the newer nurses in the group commented that hearing all the stories really made her glad she had turned down other job offers and joined this group. The affection and warmth in the group was almost palpable.

As a part of their efforts to improve teamwork and function in a more cost effective way an Idaho management team implemented "margin enhancement teams" to cut costs related to supplies and supply-related processes. In just over a year they have saved the organization over $2 million. In addition, through the teamwork around the issue of equipment they developed a Central Equipment Depot, which greatly improved employee satisfaction with the system. This large tertiary medical center regularly publishes a hospital newsletter recognizing excellence in teamwork and often has teams pictured in the newsletter celebrating their joint efforts to open a new department or make gains in customer satisfaction scores.[17]

While teamwork and camaraderie or solving high priority issues may seem to be a natural focus in health care organizations, this is not always the case. In fact, many health care facilities are textbook examples of Fire energy that is out of balance. The frenetic pace and multiple priorities often leave employees feeling anything but a sense of teamwork. It is easy to diagnose the imbalance of Fire energy when employees and managers alike complain of feeling "fried," "burned out" or, as one manager put it, "At the end of the day I feel like a gerbil on a wheel and am just exhausted."

The pace of change in health care has been a contributing factor to the scattered, frenetic environment as well as the difficulty in setting priorities. One vice president lamenting this culture norm of multiple priorities commented, "The problem is that when everything is a priority, nothing is a priority." To counter this tendency in her own management team, Mary, a Connecticut vice president, decided to have a "Pause and reflect" day in which she took her management team off-site for teambuilding. Each time the group would meet in these pause-and-reflect sessions she would ask, "What is working or not working and what do we need to do differently?" This allowed the group to step out of the frenetic pace and reflect on the ways they were using their energy as a means of regaining perspective and balance. Mary recommends this approach as a useful tool in pacing a group through a change process and staying focused on priorities. She also found it was an ideal time for the group to just have some fun and have some good "people time" with each other. She said, "I used to do this once a year, then with all the changes, I went to twice a year, now we do it every three to four months and it has really helped group morale."

Making time to get to know each other was an obvious first step for a peer group of Los Angeles department managers. They chose to meet together on a monthly basis and work on problems they had in common. In the meetings they took time for a "getting to know you activity," in which they would sit with a peer they did not know and ask them about themselves. Recently the group discovered that two managers who were sitting at the same table had been working at the facility for more than twenty years but did not know each other.

They also chose "peer partners" outside of their departments to learn more about each others' skills and talents. The directors to whom they reported had also formed a peer group to work on common issues and to develop more consistency across departments. Noting the interest his peers had in this peer group, one of the directors commented, "We have been in silos for so long that we have not really been fostering teamwork. These meetings are the first real effort we have made across silos to work together and speak with one voice." The enthusiasm in these meetings and the way in which the two peer groups were forming collaborative teams to work on issues they had in common provides a glimpse of the power of Fire energy. Not only did this effort to work together help to energize the management team, but the ramifications for employees and patients as a result of this teamwork initiative are obvious.

Patients often can benefit when teamwork and collaboration are the norm. Studies have shown that patient outcomes improve when physicians and nurses work in a collaborative way rather than an adversarial way with each other.[18] An environment of collaboration which can then foster a sense of community at work has also been shown to be a positive factor in staff retention. Kathleen, nurse manager on a spine unit, describes this environment in the article she coauthored with Jo Manion, in the *Journal of Nursing Administration*, entitled "Community in the Workplace: A Proven Strategy for Retention." She made a point of attending physician department meetings weekly and in each meeting she "highlighted" a particular staff nurse, with a picture of that person, some information about them (such as their hobbies and unique talents or their children) so that the physicians would know more about them and be sure to call them by name. Her intent was to foster personal relationships, which would then create a sense of connection and partnership.[19]

This sense of community often is felt by patients and families as well. Kathleen tells the story of Ruth, an 82-year-old patient who had been on the unit for two months while recovering from a hip fracture. She had no family or guardian and the employees treated her as if she were part of their community. She ate meals at the nurses' station and the employees "adopted" her in a way and planned recreational activities for her. When she was discharged to an adult home for the remainder of her recuperation she went through a period of transition, but eventually acclimated to this change. However when Thanksgiving Day arrived and all the other patients went home to their family, Ruth chose to return to the orthopedic unit and have Thanksgiving dinner at the nurses station with her family.

The light in Kathleen's eyes as she tells this story and the tears in the eyes of those listening remind us that the need for a sense of community is universal. Creating community at work with employees who share a sense of connection fosters a collaborative environment that is the essence of Fire energy. Just as we are drawn to a fireplace when attending a family gathering, we are drawn to the warmth and camaraderie of high-performing teams. Kathleen has a waiting list of nurses who would like to work on her unit. This is a clear testimony to the power of Fire energy.

Earth Energy—Process Improvement, Moving Away from Entitlement

One of the best ways to address Earth energy issues in the work environment is to ask the simple question: Are we busy or are we productive? All too often the honest answer is that we are just busy. Much of our business in health care comes from inattention to system problems. A Pittsburgh Medical Center recognized this in 2000 when they undertook a comprehensive study of their system issues. Gail, a senior vice president, reported they had found that nurses were spending more time nursing the system than nursing patients. In studying the work of one nurse for one hour it was found she worked in eight locations, changed locations twenty-two times, spoke to fifteen different people and spent only twenty to thirty minutes in actual time with her patient each shift.[20]

The approach they opted for to make their systems more effective was to borrow from the business world and bring in experts from Toyota to implement the "Toyota Production System." This model, which stresses rapid problem solving and work redesign, has led to significant changes in their organization at the university. They report dramatic reductions in the number of missing medications and thousands of dollars saved when nurses were no longer wasting their time in "work arounds" or moving a problem up the chain of command.[21] After three years of working with this approach their conclusion is that with adequate employee training and involvement the Toyota system can be "overlaid on the health care industry with dramatic results in improved patient care."[22]

Given the nursing shortage and the pressure to increase productivity and do more with less, it is imperative that the Earth energy issues of productivity and support be taken seriously by leaders in health care.

Another common Earth energy issue for many health care organizations involves a reluctance on the part of managers to deal effectively and decisively with marginal performers.[23] A strong sense of entitlement in the culture of health care and an organizational codependency has been fostered over the years.[24] This has been jokingly called the "bless your heart syndrome" and is typically seen in those who are not a good fit in their roles but somehow manage to be carried or taken care of by their coworkers and managers who enable the marginal behaviors. The difficulty in holding employees accountable for meeting standards of behavior has been a long-standing issue in health care. The general acceptance of codependent behaviors and an entitlement mentality are good examples of Earth energy that is out of balance.

Balanced Earth energy is evidenced in caring and supportive behavior and, as has been noted, the emotion of Earth energy is empathy. However, when the caring for another means the loss of accountability or when support becomes "they owe me," Earth energy is excessive and out of balance. Gen Xers are quick to point out their frustrations in working with "bless her heart," and this can lead to the loss of competent employees who choose to move on. A number of health care organizations have begun to address this accountability issue with the use of clinical ladders or pay for performance systems and often peer review mechanisms as well.

A Nashville hospital has combined all three of these in their approach to changing their culture. In a series of three articles for the *Journal of Nursing Administration* the authors lay out a multifaceted program, which is designed to reward clinical excellence through a clinical ladder advancement process while also collecting data for the pay for performance system.[25, 26, 27] They chose to include a component of peer review in this process as well as a self-evaluation and feedback from the manager. The clinical ladder uses Benner's novice-to-expert model as the framework for the advancement process.[28] As employee nurses are hired they are automatically placed in the clinical ladder process. In summarizing the culture changes evident in their three years of experience with this approach, they highlight an improved level of employee performance, increased accountability in both employees and managers, and an increase in coaching and mentoring behaviors.[29] Clearly this organization has chosen to invest in a culture in which professional practice is well-defined, recognized and rewarded. While the process of moving away from entitlement and getting Earth energy back in balance is labor intensive and requires constant vigilance, it has been well worth the effort. [30]

Metal Energy—
Closing a Unit, Downsizing

One of the trends in health care in this decade is the emphasis on meeting consumer expectations and on obtaining desired outcomes. This is often described as a report card mentality. Metal energy is about evaluation and standards and the importance of finishing what was started with a clear sense of mission and purpose. Managers have traditionally been taught if you want results, you need to measure and monitor. This is a key dimension of Metal energy. The health care consumer has adopted this focus on outcomes with a report card approach that has become increasingly common. Newspapers like *USA Today* and national magazines often rank hospitals based on their success rates or quality scores. Consumers are more sophisticated as they seek information that goes beyond a marketing campaign or advertisement for services. They have learned the questions to ask and are much more likely to do their homework, especially on the Internet, as they make choices about their health care. This attention on results is new for health care since for so long our emphasis had been on process rather than outcomes. As the report card mentality becomes the norm, managers and staff alike will need to shift to this outcome mindset. As Lencioni states in his best-selling book on teamwork, a key aspect of any successful team is a willingness to measure and monitor outcomes and focus on results.[31]

Another key organizational issue involving Metal energy is dealing with loss and endings effectively. Lois, an executive in a Minneapolis hospital that closed in 1991, relates a wonderful story about how the executive team in that organization made the difficult decision to close the hospital, but in a way that would be constructive rather than destructive. Their efforts, which were ultimately quite successful, provide a classic example of the wise use of Metal energy in the work environment.[32]

A key issue in Metal energy is the ability to let go of what's not working. A useful strategy in this regard is to ask hard questions as decisions are made to guide the process. In her story of this hospital closure, Lois related the essential questions that guided the work of the executive team. These included: How would the closure of departments be sequenced? How can we ensure that employees find other jobs in the system or elsewhere? How can we help physicians transition their practice to other locations? Taking the time to reflect on hard questions is fundamental to healthy Metal energy.

However, Metal energy is not only about loss but also inspiration. The executive team opted to redefine what it meant by success and focused on facilitating an ending that was as respectful, thoughtful, and value driven as possible. The team chose to go about a very difficult task in a healthy, balanced way and in so doing it reframed the experience in a way that was inspirational. The members offered employee workshops in managing transitions and dealing with the inherent grief of closure. They established a placement service for employees so that their transitions could be handled in a dignified way. They held brown bag lunches and small group meetings to answer questions and foster trust, which was a key value of the executive team.

In group meetings with employees and managers every effort was made to acknowledge the meaningful work done by individuals and groups. Many meetings ended with members applauding themselves for a job well done, which led to feeling a sense of closure. Clearly there were significant grief issues to deal with as employees prepared to move to other hospitals in the system, and employee assistance counselors were provided on an as-needed basis to assist employees and managers.

A core value in the organization had always been high-quality patient care and employees made a concerted effort to maintain their standards, monitoring activities so that there was no slippage during this transition time. Following the closure of this facility, members of the executive team received thank-you notes from employees and managers for the way they had managed this process. In reflecting on the lessons learned in this experience, Lois said, "It is the integrity of spirit that sustains us in these kinds of management challenges. You learn to focus on activities that bring value and sustain quality while trusting the process and above all keeping the faith that it will all work out."[33]

There are other examples of Metal energy issues in organizations. Metal energy is evident in a group when there is conversation around issues of personal integrity or values or spirituality. As the Michigan management team (mentioned in the Wood energy segment of this chapter) reflected on their experience with downsizing, they spoke in these terms. One of the participants in the series of meetings to cut costs commented on what it was like to see her colleagues offer their own positions for elimination or their departments to be outsourced. She remarked that it was rewarding to see the way people rose to the occasion and put the needs of the whole organization above their own needs. She felt good about the kind of people she worked with everyday and the closeness that emerged in the group.

Summary

The intent of this chapter has been to demonstrate the relevance of the Five Element Model to twenty-first century organizational life. Five energies and the functions within each of these have been discussed using specific examples from a variety of health care organizations. In previous chapters the connections of the five energies, or the Shen cycle, has illustrated the natural flow of energy from one to the next. This chapter has focused less on the flow and interrelatedness of the energies and instead looked at the energies individually. This is because in some organizations at a particular time there can be major work to be accomplished within a specific energy.

The examples offered here also illustrate the array of challenges in health care and offer some considerations for successfully addressing them. The complexity of these challenges is lessened when the functions embedded in this five thousand year old model are utilized. These functions can be used as mileposts in the design of an organization's change strategy or as evaluation guides when forward movement has stalled because of excessive or deficient energy.

No organization will ever be free of challenges, nor will there ever be a time when change stops. Our goal then is to learn how to effectively deal with these situations and stay the course to continuous improvement. Each of these situations provides us with a variety of lessons and yet another opportunity to improve the culture of our organization.

13

Increasing Personal Capacity Through Self-Care

Jo Manion and Diane Miller

A stroll in the park...or a marathon? Today's busy world presents a challenge that each of us must meet. This is the challenge of engaging in healthy self-care. The choices today on how to spend our time exist in a magnitude considered phenomenal compared to a mere one hundred years ago. Demands on our time accelerate with the increasing complexity of post-modern life. Each of us must make choices that support the flow of and encourage the replenishment of energy in our bodies and spirits. Some choose to ignore this challenge, seeing their life as a sprint. They consume their energy at a breakneck speed, only to find themselves exhausted and depleted. Others recognize that life is more like a marathon, with a need for runners to pace their expenditure of energy to be able finish the race.

This chapter explores the individual energies as a foundation for understanding aspects of self-care. In the same way the functions, found in each energy, help explain issues that must be dealt with in organizational life, so do these functions help us understand how to create a healthy sense of balance in our personal lives.

The Concept of Self-Care

Caring can be thought of as existing on a continuum, with behaviors that range from selfish to selfless with self-care in between. Selfish behavior occurs when an individual considers only his or her own needs and desires and seeks to obtain them, even at the expense of other people. Selfless behavior is when an individual gives up or disrespects his or her own needs and desires, paying attention only to the needs of others, often at her own cost. Self-care, however, is balanced within this continuum and involves recognizing your own needs and requirements, being honest about them, and then seeing that they are met. Caring for self enables one to be healthy within self and in relationships with others. People who are in service or care-giving professions, however, often engage in selfless behavior and are more likely to neglect self-care.

Sheila Collins, a professor of social work, notes that, "Caring for others is a hazardous occupation. Those of us who care for others have trouble caring for ourselves."[1] Through her work she finds that many caregivers are strong and generous people who inadvertently hurt themselves in the process of caring for others. They often give endlessly until they are exhausted and have nothing left for themselves or to give others. She encourages people in these professions to engage in self-care and believes it is a responsibility of the individual to do so.

In a survey of one thousand leaders, from first-line supervision to executive levels in organizations, I (Diane) examined the orientation about energy replenishment or self-care. In that study, only 8 percent of leaders reported a routine of self-care. I agree with Collins in her suggestion that self-care is not only a right, but a responsibility. This is especially true given the expectation that leaders are to make major decisions and maintain a balanced perspective. In the study, when self-care behavior was low, the participants exhibited tendencies of reactivity, working so quickly that solutions were ineffective and they reported feeling "empty at the end of the day."[2]

Two challenges come to bear related to self-care. The first is to find a balance between the act of supporting others with "loving kindness...and the limit-setting energy of discernment,"[3] where the individual holds back some kindness for self. The second challenge is to engage in self-care as a responsibility which has a direct positive impact on decision making and team relationships, consciously moving through feelings of guilt and avoiding slipping into chronic doing behavior.

A model for understanding key principles of self-care is found in the Five Element model, illustrated in Figure 13-1, which is used here as a framework. Examining the functions of each energy highlights the major issues for creating a life in which we pay attention to our needs and, in doing so, are able to care for others in a healthy, balanced manner.

Figure 13-1: Functions by Element

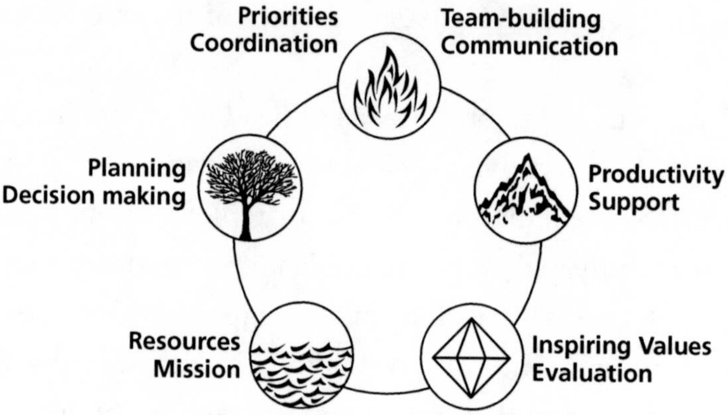

Priorities
Coordination

Team-building
Communication

Planning
Decision making

Productivity
Support

Resources
Mission

Inspiring Values
Evaluation

Source: Bellows, W. and N. Post, Functions in Groups.
Unpublished manuscript, 1987.

Water Energy

An important aspect of living a balanced life requires clarity about your purpose or your mission. Why are you here? What are you meant to accomplish or be? What is your contribution to this world? Our purpose refers to the reason for our existence. In common organizational terms, it is what we do and for whom we do it. For the individual, our sense of mission answers the question, "Why am I in this life? What do I want to give or accomplish with the time I have?" Many years ago, Stephen Covey popularized the notion of writing a personal mission statement. He believed it is a first step toward living a successful life. However, more than just a written statement, the essence of Water energy is evidenced in the reflection and consideration that goes into crafting a mission statement.

One of the most important reasons to be clear about your purpose and what you believe to be your reason for existence is that if you have a clearly defined sense of personal mission, it gives you increased clarity of direction. You know where you are going and why. A sense of mission brings focus into your life and enables you to deal more effectively with the other function of Water energy, managing your resources wisely. If you are clear about your purpose, it is easier to decline opportunities and requests that are incongruent. It allows you to say no to something that detracts you from your purpose, without feeling guilty. As a result, you are able to use your resources (energy, time, finances) most effectively.

Judicious balance or matching of these two Water functions is essential for self-care. If you see your primary purpose in this world as sharing your talents and skills in ways that are in school and have a major exam on the near horizon, you decline the invitation to go out with friends because you know you need the time to prepare. Many parents, on the other hand, delay spending money on their own desires in order to provide an education for their children. No one purpose is right or better than another. However, if you are clear about your primary purpose, it is easier to allocate resources effectively.

Another aspect of this energy is garnering the necessary resources in order to carry out your purpose. Using some of the same examples, it means investigating and having a realistic idea of what resources are necessary for you to continue your formal education. These include not only financial resources, although that is an important one, but also resources in time, energy, skill, and support. If financial resources are limited, finding alternative, less expensive ways to continue a path of formal education is realistic. Balancing the issues within this energy sometimes means making difficult choices. However, it is worth the effort because it helps you stay focused rather than allowing yourself to become distracted and fragmented.

Wood Energy

Clarity of purpose and the resources necessary to carry out that purpose is where we want to go. Wood energy is how we are going to get there. It entails seeing ourselves in a preferred future, creating for ourselves a vision toward which we strive. Both the process of defining and the holding of a vision are energizing. Our vision comes from a psychic knowing, which Beck states "will begin giving you instructions about how to reorganize the remnants of your old identity into something altogether different."[4] Having a vision for the future feeds the self, and is the basis of the hope needed to move us forward into our dreams.

Having a vision for your future is closely related to self-care. It means knowing what is possible and knowing in your heart that your future is, to a large extent, what you design it to be. Our vision of our future feeds our spirit. Self is more than just the physical body, it is our essence. It is what makes each of us the unique individual we are. The ability to see a different and desirable future for yourself gives you the ability, when coupled with action, to create that future. What do you want in your future? What are your dreams? What are your aspirations and hopes?

The second function of Wood energy is crucial because it is the action component of your vision. It is not enough to have a vision of the future; you have to put into place a structure and plan to ensure progress toward that future vision. Your vision of yourself, for example, as an independent practitioner with your own business, does not just happen. The vision must be backed up by concrete action steps that are supported by your day-to-day activities and move you forward. When you hold a clear vision of your future in your minds-eye, it helps guide your everyday actions. Beck refers to this juncture of the Wood functions as "dreaming (imagining possibilities) to scheming (planning to bring your vision to fruition)." She adds three suggestions for this endeavor: be willing to start over if your plan fails...adjust dreams and schemes to include the truths you've learned from your experimentation...and persist, continually debugging and re-implementing.[5]

An example of this was described by a woman who had gone through a very difficult, contentious divorce from her husband when their two daughters were pre-adolescents. After several years of bitterness and resentfulness, she realized that the strong animosity she held toward her ex-husband was hurting everyone involved. She decided this was not healthy for any of them. She spent a great deal of time thinking about the future. As a result, she developed a future vision for herself, her children, and her relationship with her ex-husband. The vision she began to hold was that of her and her ex dancing together at their daughters' weddings, and enjoying it! She said when she kept this picture in her head, she was able to rise above the immediate negative reactions she might have to what he was doing and how she was feeling about him, and to temper her responses in a way that brought them toward this new and very different future.

There is a multitude of examples of people who make healthy changes when they change the vision they are holding. One is the smoker who no longer sees herself as a smoker and is able to quit a decade-long smoking habit cold turkey. Another is the dieter who envisions making healthy food choices. Of course, these people are successful when their vision is backed up by a plan. How can I avoid putting myself in a situation where I might want a cigarette or the unhealthy food I desire? What action steps can I take to keep myself from becoming excessively hungry and more vulnerable to poor eating choices?

Fire Energy

Water energy is where we are headed and Wood energy is the structure that helps us determine how we are going to get there. Fire energy is the joy in life and the excitement of beginning to see results. This is when things are coming together. This energy is seen and experienced in relationships. The key functions of Fire energy relate to priority setting, coordination, communication, and relationship building. This seductive energy is aptly named because of its expansiveness and warmth.

Priority setting is a major function of Fire energy. It entails multiple aspects including sorting through a variety of options, determining which are the most likely to help you achieve the results you desire, and then ranking or assigning a value to the options in terms of their desirability. This is the essence of time management. Instead of believing that you really can do everything if you just streamline and become more efficient, you are aware that there are some things more important than others and you need to make a decision about what to do, and, perhaps more importantly, what not to do. The following story illustrates the importance of priority setting:

> A professor in his class held up a large glass jar and filled it with golf balls until they had reached the top. He asked the class, "Is the jar full?" They agreed it was. So the professor picked up a box of smaller pebbles and poured them in, shifting the jar and letting the pebbles sink down among the golf balls. He asked again, "Is the jar full?" They responded unanimously, "Yes." He then picked up a box of sand and added it to the jar. Of course, the sand filled everything else, even the tiniest nooks and crevices. Was it full? "Yes," they replied. He then added water to the jar. The students laughed.
>
> "Now," said the professor, as the laughter subsided, "I want you to recognize that this jar represents your life. The golf balls are the important things—your family, your spouse, your health, your children, your friends, your favorite passions—things that if everything else was lost and only they remained, your life would still be full. The pebbles are other things that matter, like your home, your car, your job. The sand is everything else—the small stuff. If you put the sand into the jar first, then there is no room for the pebbles or the golf balls. The same goes for your life. If you spend all your

time and energy on the small stuff, then you never have room
for the things that are important to you."

In terms of self-care, another important function of Fire energy has to do with relationships. In organizations these functions involve cooperation, coordination, communication, networking, and team building. In our personal lives, recognizing that we exist within a web of relationships and cultivating those relationships is conducive to self-care. Are the important relationships in your life energizing and healthy, or are they draining and potentially destructive? Remaining in relationships where there is a lack of trust, where respect is based on superficial attributes rather than the true substance of the individual, and where support is conditional, is not healthy. A healthy relationship also requires a high level of communication, the ability to be honest with each other, and to express yourself comfortably. The quality of your relationships has a direct impact on self-care.

One way to determine the presence of Fire energy in your life is to ask yourself, "How often do I feel joyful? Where and when do I experience a sense of joy in my life?" Joy is the emotion associated with Fire energy and it brings the sparkle to life. Daily life can be so full of demands and challenges that we forget to laugh, the voice of Fire. If you do not have people in your life with whom you laugh, look for ways to increase the laughter in your life. Watch comedy videos or sitcoms on television rather than weighty dramas. Keep a humor file of pictures, comics, funny stories or phrases. Stop reading the newspaper with its daily quota of bad news and focus on listening to and reading works that are funny and enjoyable. Do not just allow time in your day for fun, but make time in your day for fun. What do you most enjoy doing?

Celebrations are also important. This entails recognizing when something is deserving of a celebration and then making the effort to do something special. Too many times we think celebrations are reserved only for the large events of life and forget that just getting through the day sometimes deserves a celebration.

Earth Energy

Fire is expansive energy expenditure, the yang portion of the five energies. Earth is the transition element between yang and yin. It contains four functions that reflect both of these aspects, yang (producing and distributing) and yin (supporting and stabilizing). It is a "settling in" energy completing the expenditure and beginning the replenishment portions of the energy cycle.

At times it is necessary and appropriate to expend and be "out there" in the world, making things happen, bringing things together. Real-world living demands energy. In terms of self-care, one aspect is to recognize and respect that there is an ebb and flow, a cyclical rhythm to life. Earth energy provides the opportunity for a deep inhale, enjoying the bounty of the harvest, or the results of the energy spent. It is the time to sit back, let things flow over and around you. With the American emphasis of energy expenditure, entering replenishment can feel clumsy at first. Self-care is sometimes first played out as, "I just sat and did nothing," or "I just took two weeks off and vegged out on the couch." We often feel guilty about taking time for ourselves, and "away from others," as it is often stated. It is easy to experience some slipping back into "doing." The mindset to challenge is, "If we are not producing a visible external product of some kind, we are not doing anything." Reflection and replenishment are not as valued in our society, though often sought as an afterthought, and especially after burnout is encountered.

Earth energy related to self-care has to do with establishing a sense of balance and incorporating healthy patterns into daily living. Replenishment can be directed in four ways: physical, mental, emotional, and spiritual. There are several suggestions for each of these that comprise a beginning list for individualization and enhancement.

Care of the physical body is an important aspect and can begin with:

- Keeping up on current health information, as what is good for you changes quickly
- Regular exercise, including both aerobic and weight resistant exercise
- Adequate sleep and periods of relaxation during the day
- Healthy eating

Care on a mental level can begin with:
- Maintaining a healthy number of work hours with routine time away for vacation or mini-breaks
- Networking and mentoring for professional support, acquiring new knowledge

- Being with people who challenge and renew you
- Taking responsibility for clearing out negative thinking in general and in the moment of a stressful situation

Care on an emotional level can begin with:
- Building skills in coping with and managing stress
- Feeling emotions without judgment; laughing and crying as needed
- Identifying support you need from others and providing other meaningful support
- Moving into assertiveness and beyond victimization
- Exercising one of three choices in unhealthy situations: remove yourself from it, change it, or accept it totally

Care on a spiritual level, using a broad and encompassing definition, can include:
- Developing a sense of connection within your community
- Developing compassion for self (enabling self to receive love, mercy, and forgiveness) and compassion for others (for living out their humanness)
- Living in the now by totally being wherever you are at any given moment
- Accepting the process of metamorphosis (change with all of its glorious ambiguity)

Metal Energy

Metal energy, pure and distilled, is a quieter energy. Its primary functions relate to clarifying our values and living them for a life of quality. It involves recognizing those things of value and letting go of those that are less worthwhile.

The energy of Metal is clearly related to our capacity for self-care. Knowing what your values are means you are clear about what you hold dear and what is important to you, and using these as a source for day-to-day decisions. You know intuitively if you are not living a life true to your values. In some cases it is difficult to clearly know what we value most highly and it is only when we are faced with making a difficult choice that our most deeply held values are made clear. Living provides us with continuous opportunities to make choices, thus clarifying our values. In the process of clarifying, we discover both the discomfort of uncertainty, which can be the most meaningful part of decision making about our values, and the incongruence between what we value and the actions we are taking.

Many potential occasions can arise when we may say we value one thing and yet we are living a life that is not true to that value. For instance, you may say that you value integrity, yet you remain in a job situation where you are working with people who treat you disrespectfully. You may say you value honesty and yet continue to work in an organization where it is unsafe to speak honestly about situations. You may remain in a job because you believe that financial security is most important to you and continue doing work that is dissatisfying. All of these situations create a sense of dissonance, which saps your energy and makes it more difficult to live a life that is energetically full.

The first step is to continually seek deeper and deeper understanding of your values. When you feel a sense of dissonance, spend some time to reflect and understand what is causing the uncomfortable feelings. We live in such a fast-paced world with its externally focused culture and it is often difficult to listen to the silence of the inner being. Yet there are many great thinkers who recommend that we spend at least thirty-to-sixty minutes every day in a quiet, reflective activity such as meditation. For those who have never practiced this art, just sitting quietly and focusing on the present begins in minute-by-minute increments. It is work that allows our deepest feelings to surface and can help us clarify what is important in our lives.

For many of us, we may not think consciously about our values until we are faced with a crossroads in life, such as a job change, a divorce, the birth of a child, a health crisis, or loss of a loved one. There is no denying that these major life events can precipitate an increased focus on and appreciation of our values. However, living by your values is a day-to-day process, not just reserved for key turning points in your life. Living a life true to your values ensures a higher quality of life and removes the felt dissonance that arises when you live in contradiction to your values.

Another key aspect of Metal energy is letting go of those things that do not contribute to a quality life. Just as the lungs sort out the respiratory waste products and the large intestine expels digestive waste from the body, this energy allows us to eliminate those things from our life that do not bring value.

Letting go in a healthy manner is necessary for care of self. It often is not an easy process because it involves the painful emotions of grief and most of us prefer to avoid pain at all costs. The letting go may be as simple as deciding what not to spend your resources on; for example, which associations or membership groups to drop at the end of the year. Is this one bringing value into your life or just generating dozens of e-mails and mailings that are of no or little value? Is this an activity that creates some benefit in your life or are you continuing to pursue it simply because it is something you have always done?

Letting go can be as difficult as severing a long-standing relationship because it is ultimately draining your energy and hurting your life while any perceived benefit is limited. The letting go may be out of our control such as those times when we lose a loved one through death or some other event. Enduring the transition of a loving relationship from one that is in the present and reinforced by actual physical contact to one based on only memories can be very difficult. The ability to make this transition is a crucial aspect of self-care.

Summary

Balanced care of self is essential to increasing our capacity for living life to its fullest. We have only so much energy and how we choose to expend it affects the quality of our life. Choosing wisely means attending to the balance of expenditure and replenishment of our energy. It means honoring the functions of the different energies. Recognizing the role each function plays in our lives helps us make decisions that ultimately can lead to a fuller, healthier life.

14

Troubleshooting and Other Resources— at Work and at Home

Sharon Cox

Over the years of using this model, our participants and colleagues have repeatedly asked for a troubleshooting chapter to help them as they begin to apply this model in their lives, both at work and personally. This chapter is offered as a short troubleshooting manual, much like you receive with a new piece of equipment, to offer quick suggestions for getting started with a particular problem. It builds on the previous content in the book, but offers a shortcut for getting to different options.

At this point in the process of learning the Five Element model and applications to your own work setting, it is helpful to notice ways in which energy feels out of balance and then try

261

different approaches to shift the energy. Sometimes, if a group
has been floundering, this can be as simple as having a stand-
up huddle-type meeting instead of an hour-long formal
meeting with coffee and doughnuts. Often you will find that the
group is much more productive and grateful that they were
able to accomplish more in a huddle and did not waste their
time or drain their energy. The tips listed below are offered as a
frame of reference on ways you might better make use of the
meetings in which you are involved, whether in a leadership or
participant role. Typical group dynamics are mentioned as well
as suggestions on ways you might intervene.

Water Issues

Situation	Tip
Group that is floundering Meetings feel like "circling the drain"	• Develop mission statement or group charter. • Ask, "What are we here for?"

Group with low trust levels
Body language is
"shut down"
	• Deal with unresolved "old baggage"
	  from the past.
	• "Bury the old baggage" in a ritual
	  group exercise (actually put the words
	  "old baggage" on paper and then
	  tear off and put in garbage).
	• Develop ground rules for behavior as
	  a group and ways members will deal
	  with those who ignore the rules.

Low energy group
Posture is slumped or weary
Short attention span
	• Ask, "What part of this is ours to
	  own?" "What is draining your energy?"
	• Take ownership for problem solving
	  using a visual, methodical approach.
	• Move from sitting to standing
	  around a flip chart.

Group struggling with "scarcity mentality" We need to do more with less	• Clarify realistic resources, set boundaries, brainstorm possibilities, take realistic risks and "Ask for what you need."

Tips: When working with Water issues, have the group stand up around a flip chart to shift from Water to Wood energy and get some movement. Stay focused on the "circle of influence" and do not allow the group to digress into dealing with concerns over which they have no influence. It helps to draw circles on the flip chart and elicit from the group both the issues in their "circle of influence" and those that are concerns over which they have no influence. Discard the "concern" list. Also, have the group prioritize the list of things they can influence with problem-solving activities.

Wood Issues

Situation	Tip
Group has difficulty making a decision Process feels like "analysis paralysis"	• Move from conversational to visual by using flip charts or flow diagrams. • Use a methodical approach to problem solving using PDCA cycle or other problem-solving methods. Identify desired results and then do a gap analysis.
Caustic communications noted Personal attacks or judgmental responses	• Take a time out, table the issue for a future meeting, set limits or ground rules, be willing to bring consequences for inappropriate behaviors.

Group too highly structured or rigid in how they deal with issues	• Appoint a process person to monitor group process and make suggestions. • Do a "process check" at the end of the meeting to critique the meeting. • Open up the agenda for additions as the meeting begins. • Ask group for "Plan A and Plan B" to foster flexibility.
Group lacks structure and wastes time Lack of focus No sense of ownership	• Elect officers, use flip charts and develop agenda, prioritize issues. • Visually flow chart "who will do what by when" and expected results with time frames attached. Use this chart in following meetings to track progress and focus on follow-through.

Tips: Wood energy often improves when groups can get away from the work setting and gain perspective in a retreat atmosphere at least twice a year. This energy is also helped by a clear sense of big picture and game plan—otherwise they can't see the forest for the trees. It is also helpful to promote flexibility or knowing when to bend and when to take a stand. Having the group identify plan A and B and C keeps them from getting wedded to one outcome.

Fire Issues

Situation	Tip
Group is scattered and fragmented	• Decide top two or three issues with plan of action.
Multiple priorities	• Clarify roles, ask the group, "What can be delegated?"

	• Use flip charts to track the process and record the group's thinking.
Group "talks issues to death" Ineffective problem solving	• Use a methodical approach to problem solving with visual tracking of the process. Give training in brainstorming. • Define process for reaching consensus—70 percent agreement and 100 percent supportive. • Ask, "How are we helping this happen?" Take ownership for personal behavior changes.
Group has "silo" mentality Insular and territorial in dealing with issues	• Promote networking and site visits to see "best practices." • Develop cross-functional work teams and a clear expectation of interdependency.
Group is flat No sense of humor No "light in their eyes" Just going through the motions	• Encourage story telling about meaningful work the group is doing. • Be intentional about celebrating small victories and group successes (may need to rotate half group off and replace with new members annually to bring in new energy or take one meeting for self-care issues and replenishing.)

Tips: Fire energy is very seductive; it requires the facilitator to assess his or her own energy to keep from becoming part of the problem. Using flip charts and a process person to monitor group process is helpful in keeping a group on track. Off-site group activities to have fun, celebrate successes, and get to know each other foster healthy Fire energy and a sense of community at work.

Earth Issues

Situation	Tip
Workaholic patterns and martyrdom Trying to be "all things to all people"	• Clarify roles and realistic expectations. • Ask, "How are we helping this happen?" Assist the group in developing other options. • Establish mentoring or coaching relationships to provide role models.
Pervasive sense of "victim mentality" Stuck and reluctant to change	• Training on ways to deal with change and transition (Bridges Model). • Do worst-case scenarios. Site visits to see best practices. • Make the case for change with options discussed. • Make the hard decisions regarding "good fit" between the demands of the job and skill sets of the person involved.
Soap opera-like work environment Group has cliques, gossipy No boundaries between work related and personal issues	• Provide training on the impact of codependent behavior in the workplace. • Referral to employee assistance program for those with significant personal issues. • Clear expectations for teamwork and focus on patient outcomes. Motto needs to be, "Drop the drama and focus on patients and families."
Chronic problems with "support services" Basic supplies and equipment not available	• Develop structure for interdepartmental problem solving and time frames. • Set up "customer service" agreements between departments that are routinely monitored. "Fix the system rather than fixing the blame."

Tips: Earth energy relates to productivity and support; a key question to keep in mind is: "Are we just busy or are we productive?" System issues may seem overwhelming and so the option is to "work around" or blame a person when problem solving is needed instead.

Metal Issues

Situation	Tip
Difficulty letting go of past Mantra is "This is how we have always done things"	• Training in dealing with transitions. • Have a group "burial for old baggage." Regularly use the phrase, "That was then and this is now." • Interview new staff to determine their perceptions of the group's openness to new ideas.
Group lacks attention to evaluation measures and getting closure on issues	• Stress the need for personal accountability and follow-through. • Use flow charts to track group process and who will do what by when. • Post results on key indicators and recognize successes.
"Quality" is on paper only and not a routine part of the group process Concern for quality only when under pressure from accrediting groups	• Establish a system for routine audits with regular feedback to staff on results. Benchmark with other groups. • Have staff do phone interviews with patients after discharge and problem solve issues.

Inattention to "grief issues" relative to patients or peers or coping with change	• Outside resource (chaplain, CNS in Psych) to assist the group in dealing with feelings of grief. • Time off to attend to the need to regroup, if needed. • Story telling about the meaningful work done by the group as a source of inspiration.

Tips: William Bridges model on dealing with transitions provides an easy-to-use structure and process in moving from the grief of Metal energy through to Water energy and the ability to move on with a deeper sense of personal mission.

Personal Use of the Five Element Model— *Water Issues*

The body has wordless wisdom which we often call our intuitive sense, and it is important to trust that intuitive sense in relation to the need for certain energies. For instance, when you feel a need to be near the water, honor that and find a way to be near water. Drinking lots of water and adjusting one's diet to include more water-based foods (e.g., grapes, melons, etc.) can also be helpful when feeling the "pull to Water energy." Other ways to boost this energy include:

✓ Find time for quiet, peaceful time each day (fifteen to thirty minutes) to meditate or reflect on feelings in a journal or take a meditative walk (asking "What is it I need to hear?").

✓ Remember the Buddhist teaching, "Just as a jar of muddy water settles and becomes clear when it is still, so do we."

✓ Develop a healthy context for managing fear—see it as a prelude for the courage you will feel later as the process unfolds.

✓ Foster an attitude of gratitude by focusing on things you have to be grateful for. This is a wonderful way to start and end the day and will provide a noticeable shift in energy.

✓ Give some thought to things you would like to stop doing to make better use of your energy and feel more focused.

Helpful books:

Finding Your Own North Star by Martha Beck

Simple Abundance by Sarah Ban Breathnach

Wherever You Go, There You Are by Jon Kabat-Zinn

Stopping: How to Be Still When You Have to Keep Going by David Kundtz

The Power of Now by Eckhart Tolle

Wood Issues

Most often our personal issues around Wood energy relate to difficulty in making decisions or, on the other extreme, being overly critical or judgmental of ourselves and others. The latter is often the outcome when we let ourselves get "bone dry" and don't take the time to refill (Water) and replenish our spirit. The following ideas are offered in support of Wood energy and they include:

✓ Make a collage of pictures that express your personal vision.

✓ Use charts or diagrams to visually depict options or a game plan.

✓ List the top three things you are procrastinating about and choose one thing to do to get started on one of them. These "turtle steps" will get you started and foster momentum to finish the task.

✓ Get rid of clutter and get organized since clutter contributes to a sense of being overwhelmed.

✓ Finding yourself being critical or judgmental is often a symptom of a deeper issue and this needs thoughtful attention. Rather than just attending to the anger, ask what is under this (often emotional depletion) and then work on replenishing your spirit through some time off, counseling or just a chat with a good friend.

✓ Take some time away from the situation that is conflictual and you will find that getting some distance allows you to see what you need to do differently. Often just a weekend away allows you to regain perspective and be more proactive rather than reactive.

✓ Reflect on "what part of this is mine to own," and focus on personal behavior changes needed. Talk these over with a friend and make a game plan.

Helpful books:

Finding Your Own North Star by Martha Beck
Organizing From the Inside Out by Julie Morgenstern
Life Strategies by Phillip McGraw
Take Time for Your Life by Cheryl Richardson

Fire Issues

The frenetic pace of life in the twenty-first century has most of us working on ways to slow down and be present or live in the moment. All too often we find ourselves in either extreme with this energy-overdrive and then we collapse. As a result we fail to experience real joy, which is the essence of Fire energy. See which one of the tips below might help you find a better sense of balance and more fun in life.

- ✓ Take time to "schedule priorities rather than prioritizing the schedule" (Covey).
- ✓ Break big tasks down into bite-size pieces and pace yourself in the process.
- ✓ Rediscover a hobby you love or find a new one to develop your sense of creativity.
- ✓ See a funny movie or spend time with people who laugh often.
- ✓ Build a phone network of people who can help you sort out issues or problem solve situations.
- ✓ Develop a secret pal at work or just practice random acts of kindness.
- ✓ Spend time with friends who "recharge your batteries" rather than those who drain you.
- ✓ If you want to slow down, reduce caffeine or other stimulants.
- ✓ Make an effort during the day to do one thing at a time and be present.
- ✓ Listen to what your heart is telling you and act on it when possible.

Helpful books:

First Things First by Stephen Covey

The Speed Trap: How to Avoid the Frenzy of the Fast Lane
        by Joseph Bailey

The Joy Diet by Martha Beck

Don't Sweat the Small Stuff at Work by Richard Carlson

Earth Issues

Earth energy is the archetypal energy for those in the helping professions and ironically we are not at our best in this area of self-care and support. We are usually better at recommending what others need to do and fail to do those things for ourselves. If you had a care plan for yourself, what would be in that plan? Perhaps the ideas listed below will get you started on a self-care plan that is sustainable over time.

- ✓ Practice rituals that you find helpful, like having a cup of coffee and reading the paper to start your day, or listening to your favorite music on the way to work.
- ✓ Spend time with old friends who love you, "warts and all," and tell stories that bring back fond memories.
- ✓ Put fresh flowers on your desk at work or on the breakfast table.
- ✓ Get your hands in the dirt and repot a plant or tend the garden.
- ✓ Enjoy your favorite comfort foods.
- ✓ Pay a visit to a friend and thank him or her for something that person did that made a difference to you.

✓ Forgive whoever you need to—not for their sake, but for yours.

✓ Take time out to listen, really listen (or dance) to your favorite music.

✓ Have lunch at least every two weeks with a friend who nourishes you.

Helpful books:

Beyond Codependency: Getting Better All the Time by Melodie Beattie

The Dance of Anger by Harriett Lerner

Life Makeovers by Cheryl Richardson

Kitchen Table Wisdom by Rachel Naomi Remen

Metal Issues

Metal energy is about letting go of what is not working and at the same time attending to your need for inspiration. A key feature in this energy is about closure and finishing and yet how often do we find ourselves never feeling finished? As your eyes go down the list of suggestions below, notice which one speaks to you and reflect on some things you might routinely do to better manage Metal energy.

✓ On your day off choose one task you can actually finish.

✓ Clean out your closet or a file cabinet or the garage and notice how much better you feel.

✓ Choose to move on from friendships that drain and deplete your energy.

✓ See a sad movie and have a good cry now and then when you feel the need.

✓ Go to an art gallery or an exhibit or a symphony that inspires you.

✓ Listen to an inspirational speaker to remind you of the things in life that really matter, and then choose one thing you want to do differently to practice what you learned.

✓ At least quarterly, reflect in a journal or with a friend on the things in your life that are better than they were a year ago as well as lessons learned in the process.

Helpful books:

Wake Up Calls by Eric Allenbaugh

Transitions: Making Sense of Life's Changes by William Bridges

Managing Transitions: Making the Most of Change
        by William Bridges

What About the Big Stuff? By Richard Carlson

When Things Fall Apart: Heart Advice for Difficult Times
        by Pema Chodron

Changing for Good by James Prochaska

Self-Assessment Tips

Self-awareness is an essential part of using the Five Element Model in a thoughtful and effective way. How can we know what we need in the way of replenishing energy or getting ourselves back in balance? The answer to this question can be found in the Shen and K'o cycles. To recap, *if the energy is deficient, then feed it by going to the parent element on the Shen cycle* (see Figure 14-1). If Fire energy feels deficient, then move back to deal with Wood energy issues, which need to be addressed differently. If Water energy is deficient, then go back to Metal and deal with unresolved old baggage. If the energy is excessive, then balance it. Using the K'o cycle you will remember that Water puts out Fire, Fire melts Metal, Metal cuts Wood, Wood covers the Earth, and Earth holds back the Water (see Figure 14-2).

By keeping in mind this simple concept: *if it is deficient, feed it; or if it is excessive, balance it*, you will have a much better sense of what you need in your efforts for self-renewal.

Figure 14-1

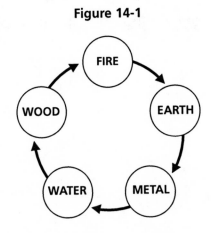

If the energy is deficient,
then feed it by going to the parent energy

Figure 14-2

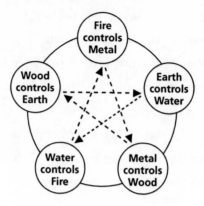

If the energy is excessive...

balance by using the opposite energy

15

Conclusion

Sharon Cox, Jo Manion, and Diane Miller

A mong the many titles we have considered for this
particular chapter were, "Gray hairs and lessons learned,"
and, "Whew!" To be perfectly honest, we also could have titled
this section, "Beginning and beginning and beginning." It has
taken us six years to write this book and begin this chapter. In
the space in between, we have experienced many moments of
personal insights about these energies within us and in the
world around us. We have found numerous ways to use the
topics covered here in our professional work as educators and
organizational consultants. Beginning with the first outline, we
faced times when it was important to renew commitment,
identify helpful processes, and obtain needed resources. We
also increased our appreciation for each other's talents and

created systems to ensure we worked well with each other. Moreover, as important as these things have been, we have discovered that writing this book has helped us each to learn more about the elegant and evolutionary aspects of this model.

This concluding chapter, on a personal and team level, merely signifies a moment in time on a continuum of understanding and appreciation of the exquisite, dynamic nature of the five energies we have discussed. Our goal here will be to honestly share how we have applied the five energies we have offered from three vantage points: personal, professional, and within this team of writers. We will also share the challenges discovered on this journey and some actions that we found helpful from which you might benefit.

Ah, Change

We have certainly encountered lessons and barriers on this journey to publication. At each twist and turn, there was always a chance to convert an obstacle into an opportunity. Holding a mindset that each of these instances was a part of the process rather than a sign the book was not meant to come to fruition was key—and always easily within our grasp. For example, in our search for a publisher we found several companies merging or changing their mission and therefore unwilling to pursue a contract for our book. Instead of being discouraged by this, we become even more determined to find a way to share this information with others. Those events became another chance to reflect on our goals and renew our intention. And, we found another way to reach our goal by self publishing. Now, and retrospectively, the phrase, "Things happen in their own time," resonates at a deeper chord for each of us. We can each see how important it is to trust the process and recognize the inherent value in the pauses that occurred in this journey, even when we become anxious about having to pause.

We have learned to respect our need to periodically suspend our writing to cope with the life events that have occurred along the way. In each of these occurrences, we discovered that we could lean into the model, relying on the wisdom of the energies to deal with the immediate stress of those situations. In fact these events influenced our writing by expanding our personal use of energies we were describing. In each case we managed these events by appreciating and attending to the energy imbalances. We now have a renewed appreciation for the need to replenish energy before acting on the next objective on our lists...and lists...and lists.

Yes, change happens. And with each change in our plan, we have been nudged back to the reality that the only constant is change. Really! So why would we presume that writing a book would be absent the steady stream of unpredictability? That is life. During one of those Oprah "light bulb moments," we discovered no one is exempt from having to deal with the ambiguity and chaos inherent in everyday living. Not even authors! With each change we found our individual and collective ability to regroup, reframe, revisit, and rewrite. Our belief in the fluid nature of planning came to the forefront each time something we had designed dissolved into bits and pieces. We have learned to trust our creative capacity to identify alternatives, modeling these into plan B, C, etc. With each change, we found another time to practice what we were teaching. Each time we honed even more our ability to switch gears or identify a different way to achieve a goal.

One of the predictable things about our work was that we would rarely be in the same room with each other. This could have thrown a great big monkey wrench into our plan and limited our success. In six years we three have been together on only one occasion. It is simply the reality of the lives we lead. We have often laughed about waving to each other at thirty thousand feet while we were each headed to yet another client. This is also a true reflection of the reality our colleagues, friends, and family experience. How often have we heard that getting a whole team together at one time for anything feels like herding cats! So, we had to avoid the temptation to build a process on a foundation of unrealistic time expectations. That is a primary issue today—virtual teams is the name of the game! Thankfully, we found ways to operate within this resource boundary, being sure our productivity was not contingent on being in the same room with each other. Instead, we connected electronically. We also gave each other encouragement when a deadline needed to be extended or when the pangs of guilt struck yet again.

We recognized our own need to connect and the benefit of consulting with each other. In conversations we often spoke about the clarity, simplification, and synergy we felt after talking things over with each other. We used that approach to get on the page with each other, moving through conflicting perspectives before those turned into wedges in our process or our relationships. Our calls to each other were purposeful. Sometimes these were about seeking help.

And, we were typically sensitive to each other's priorities and pressures. Our lifeline with each other was a prop when we floundered. It was a source of support when energy or focus began to flag a bit. It kept each of us honest and goal-oriented. Sometimes we shared a "dah" about something we had missed. These were also opportunities to remind each other to take ourselves less seriously in this process of seriously pursuing our goal of authoring this book.

Professional Reflections

As mentioned earlier, each of us greatly increased our understanding of the five energies during the writing of this book. Despite our collective experience of several decades with this model, we have each realized that assuming the role of author is both a humbling and growth-fostering experience. Over the course of our journey we amassed file folders filled with information, books, ideas, and notes. We have a collection of more floppy disks filled with early drafts than we might wish to admit! We have sketched thoughts on countless sheets of paper and napkins while having lunch. And the lesson in all of that is: too many resources can be as much a limitation as too few. We shifted through trivial to find the pearls of wisdom we wanted to share. At other times, we stretched ourselves into a new "Aha" about this model or about ourselves. So, writing this book required embracing the counterintuitive, making less from more.

The specific challenge was distilling all we wished to share into essential segments, principles, and practices. Attention needed to be given to theory while also honoring the fundamental, diverse needs of adult learners who are hungry for applications of the new learning. We recognized that some readers would seek out the why behind the information, others would want facts. Some would want to dream while having total autonomy about the aspects of the material that fit their personal and professional lives. That sometimes felt like too much diversity. Pulling up our shirt sleeves, we dove into balancing detail with brevity. We adopted a mantra of communicating in a meaningful, practical, and user-friendly way. We were compelled to continually identify what really mattered from our vantage point and the reader's. We needed to harness our enthusiasm, holding it short of evangelism. With each chapter we wrote, we were more aware of the nuances, the depth, and the intuitive logic of the five energies. And these bolstered our belief that this five-thousand-year-old model is applicable today and into the future.

Once we set our sights on sharing this model, we seemed to see the model everywhere. This is not unlike wanting to buy a particular model of car and then noticing everyone and his brother seems to be driving that one! With each observation of an energy, we also found yet another example to share. With another dose of critical thinking, we looked for the best ways to illustrate points made from the plethora of case studies that became available to us. With each situational observation of the five energies, we renewed our collective commitment to continuous learning. Our appreciation of the continual flow of energies within groups and organizations was constantly renewed. By sharing these insights with each other, we added to our collective intelligence and supported each other in mentoring ways prior to, during or after consultative visits. By teaching this material over the course of our writing, we increased the depth of our understanding and refined our approaches over time. This practice helped us in stating the model more succinctly in our own minds, which influenced the ways we eventually captured it in these pages. Simply by committing to teach this material, we were creating a positive reinforcement cycle that propelled us forward.

Having to knowledgeably present this material has been a great catalyst for our continued, on-going learning about our subject matter. Some of the learning came in blinding flashes of the obvious. Others came in a more subtle "Aha!" wave moving through a room of seminar participants. There have been times when we articulated an aspect of this discussion in a memorable way with each other, registering those examples for use here. With our increased focus on the material, we repeatedly discovered other applications in our own practices. This further heightened our interest and underlined our intention to write. As teachers of this material on a continuous learning curve, we experimented more boldly. With each use, our competence increased. And in each of these examples, we also discovered the gaps in our understanding.

Personal Reflections

This section could be headed, "Practice what we preach!" It points to two of the principles of effectiveness in using the five energies in groups. The first is that effectiveness requires embracing these energies on a personal level. Second, one's personal energy needs to be balanced before acting on an energy issue noticed within a group. This can be termed, "working from the inside to the outside." There are many other models that also work best using this approach. As an example, empowerment truly begins when one understands authority and assertiveness on a personal level and then applies that knowledge in organizational context. Leadership, demonstrated on a personal level, informs effectiveness in that competence within an organization. We understand that our personal competency with these energies creates the basis for our authenticity. And as we are willing to walk the talk of this model, we also shore up our credibility within these pages and in our consulting practices.

Yet, practicing what we preach has not been a risk-free endeavor. It required our continuous and honest evaluation of our energy state. Among the areas we had to consider in our personal appraisal were:

- Actively addressing competency gaps in our own ability to balance personal energy
- Consciously carrying out a plan to balance energies that are deficient or excessive
- Knowing self supports the identification of good questions to ask about the five energies
- Building personal competency with the five energies by intentional noticing
- Achieving success by balancing the five energies in our work
- Growing in our awareness and use of The Law of Least Action

These areas are all addressed here briefly.

Actively addressing competency gaps in our own ability to balance personal energy

To be successful, we each needed to build a personal working knowledge of the five energies. Two aspects of this commitment are: being able to read cues in our physical, emotional, and spiritual self as well as building a workable set of action tools that can be taken to address energy imbalances. We also needed to attend to our personal energy in creating "to-do" lists in general and adding our writing responsibilities to those lists. We sometimes had to say we needed to take time for other things in our lives. On occasion we needed to nudge each other to set aside our writing duties for a period of time until personal balance and focus were restored.

Consciously carrying out a plan to balance energies that are deficient or excessive

Too often, we acknowledged things were off center or compared notes on those things that were consuming our energies. With that acknowledgment we assertively acted to address the excesses or deficiencies. We overcame our tendency to problem-process by moving into proactive decision making in those situations. We caught ourselves and each other allowing the imbalance to continue or play out in an unhealthy way. We improved in taking action on cues that it was time to slow down, replenish energy, or control an excess energy.

Knowing self supports the identification of good questions to ask about the five energies

Among the many questions we asked in our process were:

- What are my traps and vulnerabilities?
- Are there specific energies that I over- or underutilize?
- Are there activities in this process that seem to come easily for me?
- What are my options to balance myself?
- What can I learn from others about using this model for my personal health?
- What are some of the innate strengths I can offer to this team endeavor?
- What are the specific activities that stretch for me in this process, and are there also times when things have gone easily?

With each question, we came to know ourselves better. By sharing our answers, we came to understand even more about the beauty of our diversity as a team. We also offered additional questions or feedback when those things seemed appropriate. The richness of our strengths helped us direct efforts more effectively.

Building personal competency with the five energies is enhanced by intentional noticing

Noticing is best done in quiet, still reflection to be better able to hear the answers. In our conversations with each other, we clarified our specific energy patterns, imbalances, and ways to address those imbalances. We have shared the physical and emotional sense of the energies, honing our ability to articulate these components for others. We have increased our honesty about the need to actively manage our own energy and using feedback from each other about additional strategies that could be effective. Broadening our personal experience with the energies was invaluable in the writing of this book and increased our ability to translate this material into real-life applications.

One of the key principles of this model reminds us to ensure that personal energy is addressed before intervening on an energy issue in a group. If the facilitator is not balanced, the assessment or intervention can be inaccurate. The assessment of self follows the observation for imbalance in a group and precedes acting on that assessment information. The principle, then, is articulated in a specific sequence that needs to be honored to have a beneficial result: Observe, Adjust self, Observe again, Intervene.

The logic here is to ensure that actions taken to address energy issues in a group actually match the group's energy need rather than the energy needs of the facilitator. Too many times, the "adjust self" step is overlooked. Too often, a reaction to the situation rather than a thoughtful assessment of what the need truly is takes place. As facilitators, we revisited the elegance of that four-step process. In the process of writing this book, we have confronted this need to consciously assess our own energy states before sending edits to each other or as we were developing plans for specific situations. Have we perfected our personal competency with the five energies? The answer is a resounding no. Are we more assertive in our personal process? The answer is more yes than no. It is, after all, a process and on some days we were more diligent and skilled than on others.

The Five Energy model is as vulnerable as other models, including Myers-Briggs, Jung or Human Dynamics, to being used to label. We remained mindful of that pitfall in our organization of responsibilities within our team. Stereotyping breaks the essential and complementary nature of this model. While it might have been easy to relegate activities to the team member who was strongest in the specific energy, we were aware that would have made that individual the container for that energy. Instead we believed our effectiveness was contingent on each member building competency across a wide range of activities. Our decision to mutually share in responsibilities certainly was to the benefit of the whole team and seemed intrinsically better than aligning activities in the team with our individual, primary energies. We actively brought and utilized our innate, individual capacity. Sometimes that meant staying in the struggle with activities rather than giving it on to another member of the team. We asked for each others' perspective and feedback when we were unsure we had achieved a desired goal. That not only raised our personal competency, but also increased the level of synergy we experienced in our team.

Growing in our awareness and use of the Law of Least Action

The Law of Least Action emphasizes the power of subtlety. It is one of the operating guidelines of this model that we have most often revisited. Rather than using great big, dramatic fanfare framed in glitz approaches, the Law of Least Action is the gentle nudge that creates forward movement. Western thinking, especially in the US, often leans to the flamboyant. At times it is an ego-laden action that can be worded as, "Let me tell you what I know," which can be followed with, "You poor, pitiful ___." Western practitioners sometimes play out this arrogance in interactions with the clients they serve and the staff they manage.

We have approached this writing journey with a goal of sharing information, not from our vantage point but the perspective of the reader. In this venture as in our work with the model in groups over the years, we began with the understanding that these individuals already had an intuitive knowledge of the energy model. Our primary opportunity was to build the awareness in breadth and depth. In the past we have chosen to work in a collaborative exploration, using examples from their lives, the teams they work with or their organizations. We were also aware of the need to get over being a consultant. With that decision we were able to avoid the tendency to talk at or teach from a, "Here, let me give you this piece of information."

This Law of Least Action requires beginning with what is known, in this case, our clients' innate and intuitive understanding of aspects of this model. We repeatedly asked ourselves and our clients about their real issues, the situations they struggled with. We approached content from the "Aha moments" when a description or an analogy helped a group apply the construct of these energies.

We held the goal of assisting readers to see the essential simplicity of the model rather than grooming individuals to become facilitators responsible for using this model in their organization. That lightened our touch and directed our energies.

And there were opportunities to use the Law of Least Action within our team. When our energy for this work waned, we adjusted priorities or time lines rather than pushing forward or forcing effort. When we had conflicting perspectives or unmet needs, we simply discussed those situations rather than letting them become larger issues. We gave ourselves some time away, working on any guilt we might have felt about not getting that next item off the to-do list. Being goal-oriented consultants, this relaxed, subtle approach was a welcome change of pace. By doing this we could attend to the immediate issues and write when we could do so in a focused and productive way.

Lessons Learned About Our Virtual Team

Honoring the symmetry of the energy model was the first and potentially the most important lesson learned in the writing of this book. Practically speaking, it takes all five energies for harmony. The universe around us is an everyday reminder of healthy balance and harmony. The awareness of the symmetry of the model eventually influences us in making choices about the team of authors who would join together on this project. Yes, there were a few false starts, a few critical things that were initially overlooked and eventually corrected.

Our team needed to consciously attend to both the completion of the work and our relationships with each other. All teams are tempted to or unconsciously fail to appreciate the whole of that equation. For instance, the intensity of the work can become the central focus to the extent that how we work with each other is overlooked. The converse can also be the case, committing time to simply being with each other without making decisions about what the work is or expecting pages to be produced has an equal, negative result.

How we produced content was the subject of numerous discussions. We discussed times when an idea seemed to magically come to us with little or no effort. We shared how we struggled with a particular section. We learned to appreciate how much comes of unattended processing, perhaps our best example of the Law of Least Action. Those effortless insights came to us while traveling, while working on something vastly different than the subject we were exploring, and sometimes in the shower. We discussed the need to wait for the words to come to us rather than forcing the process. At times a life event required one of us to temporarily suspend work on the book. Sometimes we needed to stop because our efforts were non-productive. At other times we needed to attend to a barrier before we could move forward. All of us entered this project with positive and negative experience with writing. Open discussions of those historic difficulties were important. Talking about how to overcome that history was often the first step in the right direction.

We each needed to trust in the intention of the other members of the team. Honoring each other's past experience and specific strengths was most helpful. Balancing independence and interdependence in this process was key. This specifically meant respecting that we would be working autonomously while also benefiting from thinking with each other. We individually wrote sections of this book, being careful to also identify points of consistency that were needed for a cohesive flow. While no individual on our team was identified as the leader, we all recognized how essential it was to coordinate and collaborate.

How We Applied the Five Element Model to Our Own Work

Perhaps the greatest lesson was that our knowledge of the model was strengthened by applying the five energies and twelve functions to our writing and team process. Table 15-1 describes the specific functions of the five energies and how we used these to enhance effectiveness. This table demonstrates the usefulness of this model in both designing work and overcoming obstacles. The model gave us a needed infrastructure without being so structured or complex that it limited our success.

Table 15-1: Applying the Model to Our Work

Element	Issues	Actions
Water	Clarify purpose	• What is my goal in this chapter?
		• What do I want to achieve?
		• What are my main points?
		• What resources do I have or need for this section?
		• Do I have the time right now to do this writing and be effective?
	Intention	• Appreciating the power of our individual and collective motivation to write this book
		• Frequently revisiting our commitment

Element	Issues	Actions
	Resource	• Including personal time, talent to support forward movement
	Trust	• The subjective faith that the process would flow (be evolutionary in nature)
		• Positive belief in each other's intentions
Wood	Vision	• Keeping a mental picture of the completed product
	Planning	• Establishing a process for getting materials back and forth and reviewing each other's work
		• Determining responsibility for each section
	Time management	• Setting timelines that were neither too ambitious nor too ambiguous
		• Avoiding framing expectations in a way that increased pressure
Fire	Coordination	• Creating systems needed to initiate and sustain efforts
		• Merging clear focus and vision (Wood) with critical thinking and the ability to work in concert (Fire)
	Priorities	• Stating clearly and following through
		• Using water to balance fire, thus avoiding random efforts
		• Recommitting to this process, unifying intention to increase energy
	Communication	• How to best handle this given our physical separation?
		• How often did we need to touch base with each other?

Element	Issues	Actions
	Building a functional team	• Agreeing on a group of three but acknowledging there were a number of partnerships based on what we need to accomplish
		• Using the structure needed at the time
		• Using mentoring behaviors with each other
		• Choosing collaborating rather than competing
		• Keeping our collective eye on the goal: getting the information into a useful form so that others can learn
		• Recommitting (continually) to help each other
		• Using the superficial circulation (of functions 1 and 2 of Fire) too reignite our purpose, commit our personal resource (function 3 of Water energy)
		• Listening and sharing ideas, addressing conflict versus allowing these to become a barrier, building respect and support with each other
Earth	Production	• Balancing goals/expectations with resources
		• Working when time was right/when energy was balanced
		• Asking how do I work best? What are supportive rituals and patterns I can use?
		• Recognizing that "overworked" (Earth) impacts achieving purpose (Water)

Element	Issues	Actions
	Ensuring needed systems were available	• Getting beyond writer's block • Overcoming perfectionism by becoming comfortable asking for and receiving feedback • Breaking down whole chapters into sections that were achievable • Mind-mapping ideas and brainstorming to increase creativity • Moving from energy into synergy by partnering with each other • Celebrating success as we go
Metal	Evaluating	• Continuously looking for opportunities to refine
	Eliminating	• What do we keep and get rid of (content)? • Addressing loss of energy • Deciding when it was best to let it go (setting the project aside, temporarily)
	Celebrating	• Taking time to recognize successes, intentionally

We found that it is not uncommon these days to enter into discussions about the meaning of the work we undertake or to consider ways to make that work more meaningful in the future. Of equal importance is considering how work can and does provide us with lessons about how we relate to others. In each of these opportunities, we can fine-tune our emotional and relational competencies.

In the process of writing this book and with reliance on the body of knowledge we have shared, we have overcome barriers and enjoyed success together. We have a deeper appreciation for each other because we have committed to a unified vision. We have each grown on an individual and a team level because we were willing to stretch ourselves and each other.

Our success was contingent upon our recognizing the need to honor what we were writing about. Among all the changes we experienced, the one thing that was predictable and ever present were the five energies and the flow of these energies in the Shen cycle. This process has also been ambiguous, uncertain, and unpredictable. We have encountered the need to balance and control energies along the way, in the moment, and repeatedly. It is impossible to list during a planning process when imbalances will be encountered. What can be outlined is that imbalance will need to be addressed and how to address these.

At this juncture, it is reasonable to ask whether the energy we invested was worthwhile. On a personal level, each of us learned something. That is the gift we received for the investment we have made. Professionally speaking, the effort we dedicated to exploring, researching, and articulating the facets of the Five Energy model has resulted in informing our consultative practices. As a team, we have enjoyed laughter and celebrated successes. We can proudly identify numerous obstacles we have successfully circumvented and managed in real time. We have each grown in our respect for each other with each section we have produced. If we can say nothing more than these things in answering whether our investment in this project was worthwhile, then we have said a mouthful!

Endnotes

Preface

1. *Newsweek*: The Science of Alternative Medicine, "Health for Life," Dec. 2, 2002: 45.

Chapter 1: What is the Five Element Model?

1. G. Reichstein, *Wood Becomes Water: Chinese Medicine in Everyday Life* (New York: Kodansha International, Inc., 1998).

2. A. Eckert, *Chinese Medicine for Beginners* (Rocklin, CA: Prima Publishing, 1996).

3. J. Elias and K. Ketcham, *In the House of the Moon: Reclaiming the Feminine Spirit of Healing* (New York: Warner Books, 1995).

4. H. Beinfield and E. Korngold, *Between Heaven and Earth: A Guide to Chinese Medicine* (New York: Ballantine Books, 1991).

5. Elias and Ketcham, *In the House of the Moon*.

6. Ibid.

7. Ibid., *Reclaiming the Spirit of Healing*, 78.

8. Ibid.

9. Ibid.

10. Nancy Post, "Elements of Organization" training program lecture notes (Philadelphia, 1993).

11. Beinfield and Korngold, *Between Heaven and Earth*, 112.

12. Eckert, *Chinese Medicine for Beginners*.

13. Beinfield and Korngold, *Between Heaven and Earth*, 87.

14. E. Haas, *Staying Healthy With the Seasons* (Berkeley, CA: Celestial Arts, 1981).

15. Eckert, *Chinese Medicine for Beginners*, 12.

16. Ibid, 3.

17. D. Degraff, *The Body Owner's Manual—An Acupuncturist's Teachings on Health and Well Being* (New York, NY: Berkley Books 1998), 37.

18. D. Connelly, *Traditional Acupuncture: The Law of the Five Elements*, 2nd ed. (Columbia, MD: Traditional Acupuncture Institute 1994).

19. Reichstein, *Wood Becomes Water*, 12.

20. Elias and Ketcham, *Chinese Medicine for Maximum Immunity: Understanding the Five Elemental Types for Health and Well Being* (New York: Three Rivers Press, 1998), 4.

Chapter 2: Apply the Model to Modern Organizational Life

1. Post, "Managing Human Energy: An Ancient Tool of Change Experts," *OD Practitioner* (December 1989): 14.

2. Post, "Elements of Organization" training program lecture notes, Philadelphia, 1993.

Chapter 3: Organizing Principles

1. Reichstein, *Wood Becomes Water*.

2. Post, "Elements of Organization."

3. Reichstein, *Wood Becomes Water*.

4. Post, "Elements of Organization."

Chapter 4: Water

1. Connelly, *Traditional Acupuncture*, 75.

2. Elias and Ketcham, *Chinese Medicine for Maximum Immunity*, 124.

3. Hammer, *Dragon Rises, Red Bird Flies: Psychology and Chinese Medicine* (Barrytown, NY: Station Hill Press, 1990), 9.

Chapter 5: Wood

1. Beinfield and Korngold. *Between Heaven and Earth*, 134.

2. Post, course notes, 1993.

3. Elias and Ketcham, *Chinese Medicine for Maximum Immunity*, 30.

4. L. Bilodeau, *The Anger Workbook*, Hazeldine, 9.

5. Elias and Ketcham, *Chinese Medicine for Maximum Immunity*, 24.

6. Ibid., 25.

7. Warren Bellows, *Functions in Groups*, unpublished.

8. Beinfield and Korngold, *Between Heaven and Earth*, 173.

9. Elias and Ketcham, *Chinese Medicine for Maximum Immunity*, 23.

Chapter 6: Fire

1. Elias and Ketcham, *In the House of the Moon*, 112.

2. V. Kast, *Joy, Inspiration, and Hope* (New York: Fromm International Publishing Corporation, 1994), 16.

3. Ibid, 4, 5.

4. C.E. Izard, *The Psychology of Emotions* (New York: Plenum Press, 1991), 132.

5. C.E. Izard, "Organizational and Motivational Functions of Discrete Emotions," *Handbook of Emotions* (New York: The Guilford Press, 1993), 634.

6. Ibid., *The Psychology of Emotions*, 138.

7. Kast, *Joy, Inspiration, and Hope*, 46.

8. Ibid., 43.

9. J. Pittam and K.R. Scherer, "Vocal Expression and Communication of Emotion," *Handbook of Emotions*, Lewis and Haviland, Eds. (New York: The Guilford Press, 1993), 631-641.

10. Reichstein, *Wood Becomes Water*, 64.

11. Elias and Ketcham, *In the House of the Moon*, 109.

Chapter 7: Earth

1. Elias and Ketcham, *Chinese Medicine for Maximum Immunity*.

2. Ibid.

3. Reichstein, *Wood Becomes Water*.

4. Elias and Ketcham, *Chinese Medicine for Maximum Immunity*.

5. Ibid.

6. Q. Studer, "From Customer Satisfaction to Bottom Line Results," presentation for American Organization of Nurse Executives annual meeting, March 2002, Nashville, TN.

7. Elias and Ketcham, *Chinese Medicine for Maximum Immunity*, 91.

Chapter 9: Diagnosis and Intervention

1. Beinfield and Korngold, *Between Heaven and Earth*, 132.

2. E. Ross-Krieger, "The Wisdom of Chinese Medicine: A Powerful, Practical Paradigm for Organizational Development Practitioners" unpublished manuscript (Walnut Creek, California, 1994), 5.

3. Connelly, *Traditional Acupuncture*, 2nd ed., 1994, 116.

Chapter 10: Mastering Change

1. J. Flowers, "Being Effective," *Healthcare Forum Journal*, 34(3) (1991): 53.

2. D.T. Phillips, *Lincoln on Leadership: Executive Strategies for Tough Times* (New York: Time Warner Books, 1992).

3. J. George Wilson and R. Wellins, *Leadership Trapeze: Strategies for Leadership in Team-Based Organizations* (San Francisco: Jossey-Bass Publishers, 1994).

4. W. Bridges, *Managing Transitions: Making the Most of Change* (New York: Addison Wesley, 1991).

Chapter 12: Contemporary Organizational Challenges

1. Q. Studer, "Taking Your Organization to the Next Level," Presentation for Tenet Health Care System Southeastern Region Nurse Administrators, June 20, 2002.

2. L. Whisman, "Creating a Culture of Service Excellence," Presentation for Franklin Square Medical Center, June 14, 2002.

3. Ibid.

4. Studer, "Taking Your Organization to the Next Level"

5. Whisman, L. "Creating a Culture of Service Excellence"

6. Ibid.

7. Ibid.

8. Ibid.

9. T. Porter-O'Grady "Is Shared Governance Still Relevant?" *Journal of Nursing Administration*, October 2001, 468.

10. K. Stolzenberger, K. "Beyond the Magnet Award" *Journal of Nursing Administration*, October, 2003, 522.

11. Porter-O'Grady "Is Shared Governance Still Relevant," 468.

12. M. Jenkins, "Shared Decision Making," Presentation for Genesys Regional Medical Center, June 13, 2003

13. Ibid.

14. Ibid.

15. Ibid.

16. P. Lencioni, *The Five Dysfunctions of a Team* (San Francisco: Jossey-Bass, 2002)

17. K. Michelletti, "Keeping in Touch Employee Newsletter," St. Alphonsus Medical Center, Boise Idaho. Volume 5, Issue 10, March, 2004

18. J.G. Baggs et al., "Association Between Nurse-Physician Collaboration and Patient Outcomes in Three Intensive Care Units," *Journal of Critical Care Medicine*, 27, no. 9 (September, 1999).

19. J. Manion and K. Bartholomew, "Community in the Workplace: A Proven Retention Strategy," *Journal of Nursing Administration* (January, 2004).

20. D. Thompson, et al., "Driving Improvement in Patient Care: Lessons from Toyota," *Journal of Nursing Administration* (January 2004).

21. Ibid.

22. Ibid., 595.

23. P. Neuhauser, "Building a High Retention Culture in Healthcare," *Journal of Nursing Administration* (September, 2002).

24. D. Noer, Healing the Wounds (San Francisco: Jossey-Bass, 1993).

25. K. Robinson, C. Eck, B. Keck, and N. Wells, "The Vanderbilt Professional Nursing Practice Program, Part One," *Journal of Nursing Administration* (September, 2003): 441.

26. N. O'Hara, M. Duvanich, M. Foss, and N. Wells, "The Vanderbilt Professional Practice Program, Part Two," *Journal of Nursing Administration* (October, 2003).

27. R. Steahan, et al., "Vanderbilt Professional Nursing Program— Part Three," *Journal of Nursing Administration* (November, 2003).

28. P. Benner, *From Novice to Expert: Excellence and Power in Clinical Nursing Practice* (Menlo Park, California: Addison-Wesley, 1984).

29. R. Steahan, R. et al., "Vanderbilt Professional Nursing Program—Part Three," *Journal of Nursing Administration* (November, 2003).

30. Ibid.

31. P. Lencioni, *The Five Dysfunctions of a Team* (San Francisco: Jossey-Bass, 2002).

32. L. Hybben-Stehr, *"The Human Side of a Hospital Closure"* unpublished manuscript, June, 2001.

33. Ibid., 8.

Chapter 13: Increasing Personal Capacity through Self-Care

1. S.K. Collins, *Stillpoint: The Dance of Self-caring, Self-healing* (Fort Worth, TX: TLC Productions, 1992), 5.

2. D. Miller, *Defining Self-Renewal For Leaders: Application of the Chinese Medical Model.* Unpublished Masters Thesis, 1996, 30.

3. E. Frankle, "Sweetening the Judgments," *Parabola: Myth, Tradition and the Search for Meaning* (Spring 2003): 19.

4. M. Beck, "Transformation," *Oprah Magazine*, January, 2004, 140.

5. Ibid., 170.

Bibliography

Allenbaugh, E. *Wake Up Calls: You Don't Have to Sleepwalk Through Life.* Austin, TX: Discovery Publications, 1991.

Baggs, J.G., and M. Schmidt, A. Mushlin, P. Mitchell, D. Eldredge, D. Oakes, A. Hutson. "Association Between Nurse-Physician Collaboration and Patient Outcomes in Three Intensive Care Units." *Journal of Critical Care Medicine*, 27, no. 9 (September, 1999): 991.

Bailey, J. *The Speed Trap: How to Avoid the Frenzy of the Fast Lane.* San Francisco: Harper Books, 1999.

Ban Breathnach, S. *Simple Abundance*. New York: Warner Books, 1995.

Beattie, M. *Beyond Codependency: Getting Better All the Time.* New York: Harper and Row, 1989.

Beck, M. *Oprah Magazine*. "Transformation." January 2003.

_____. *Finding Your Own North Star.* New York: Three Rivers Press, 2001: 140, 170.

_____. *The Joy Diet: 10 Practices for a Happier Life.* New York: Crown Publishers, 2003.

Bellows, W., and N. Post. *Functions in Groups.* Unpublished manuscript, 1987.

Beinfield, H., and E. Korngold. *Between Heaven and Earth: A Guide to Chinese Medicine.* New York, NY: Ballantine Books, 1991.

Benner, P. *From Novice to Expert: Excellence and Power in Clinical Nursing Practice.* Menlo Park, California: Addison Wesley, 1984.

Bilodeau, L. *The Anger Workbook*. Minneapolis: Hazeldine, 1992.

Bridges, W. *Managing Transitions: Making the Most of Change*. New York: Addison Wesley, 1991.

_____. *Transitions: Making Sense of Life's Changes*. New York: Addison Wesley, 1980.

Carlson, R. *Don't Sweat the Small Stuff at Work*. New York: Hyperion, 1998.

_____. *What About the Big Stuff?* New York: Hyperion, 2002.

Chia, M., and M. Chia. *Fusion of the Five Elements*. Huntington, NY: Healing Tao Books, 1989.

Chodron, P. *When Things Fall Apart: Heart Advice for Difficult Times*. Boston: Shambhala Press, 1997.

Collins, S. K. *Stillpoint: The Dance of Self-caring, Self-healing*. Fort Worth, TX: TLC Productions, 1992.

Connelly, D. *Traditional Acupuncture: The Law of Five Elements*. Columbia, Maryland: The Center for Traditional Acupuncture, 1979.

_____. *Traditional Acupuncture: The Law of Five Elements*, 2nd Edition. Columbia, Maryland: The Center for Traditional Acupuncture, 1994.

Covey, S. *The Seven Habits of Highly Effective People*. New York: Simon & Schuster, 1989.

_____. *First Things First*. New York: Simon & Schuster, 1994.

Cox, S. *Managing the Workplace 2000*. Unpublished manuscript, 1996.

Degraff, D. *The Body Owner's Manual: An Acupuncturist's Teachings on Health and Well Being*. New York: Berkley Books, 1998.

Eckert, A. *Chinese Medicine for Beginners*. Rocklin, CA: Prima Publishing, 1996.

Elias, J. and K. Ketcham. *Chinese Medicine for Maximum Immunity: Understanding the Five Elemental Types for Health and Well Being*. New York: Three Rivers Press, 1998.

_____. *In the House of the Moon: Reclaiming the Feminine Spirit of Healing*. New York: Warner Books, 1995.

Flowers, J. "Being Effective." *Healthcare Forum Journal*, 34, no. 3 (1991): 52–57.

Frankle, E. "Sweetening the Judgments," *Parabola: Myth, Tradition and the Search for Meaning*, Spring 2003.

Haas, E. *Staying Healthy With the Seasons*. Berkeley, CA: Celestial Arts, 1981.

Hammer, L. *Dragon Rises, Red Bird Flies: Psychology and Chinese Medicine.* Barrytown, NY: Station Hill Press, 1990.

Hybben-Stehr, L. "The Human Side of a Hospital Closure." Unpublished manuscript, June, 2001.

Izard, C.E. *The Psychology of Emotions.* New York: Plenum Press, 1991.

———. "Organizational and Motivational Functions of Discrete Emotions." In M. Lewis & J.M. Haviland (Eds.) *Handbook of Emotions.* New York: The Guilford Press, 1993.

Jenkins, J. *Advanced Practice Nursing Quarterly* 1, no. 4 (1996).

Jenkins, M. "Shared Decision Making." Presentation for Genesys Regional Medical Center, June 13, 2003.

Kabat-Zinn, J. *Wherever You Go, There You Are.* New York: Hyperion Press, 1992.

Kaptchuk, T. *The Web That Has No Weaver.* New York: Congdon & Weed, 1983.

Kast, V. *Joy, Inspiration, and Hope.* New York: Fromm International Publishing Corporation, 1994.

Kundtz, D. *Stopping: How to Be Still When You Have to Keep Going.* Berkeley, CA: Conari Press, 1998.

Lencioni, P. *The Five Dysfunctions of a Team.* San Francisco: Jossey-Bass, 2002.

Lerner, H. *The Dance of Anger,* New York: Harper and Row, 1986.

McGraw, P. *Life Strategies: Doing What Works—Doing What Matters.* New York: Hyperion, 1999.

Manion, J., and K. Bartholomew. "Community in the Workplace: A Proven Retention Strategy." *Journal of Nursing Administration* (January 2004): 46–53.

Michelletti, K. "Keeping in Touch Employee Newsletter," St. Alphonsus Medical Center, Boise, Idaho. Volume 5, Issue 10, March, 2004.

Miller, D. *Defining Self-Renewal For Leaders: Application of the Chinese Medical Model.* Unpublished Masters Thesis, 1996.

Morgenstern, J. *Organizing From the Inside Out,* New York: Henry & Holt, 1998.

Neuhauser, P. "Building a High Retention Culture in Healthcare." *Journal of Nursing Administration* (September, 2002): 470–478.

Newsweek. The Science of Alternative Medicine, "Health for Life." Dec. 2, 2002: 45.

Noer, D. *Healing the Wounds*, San Francisco: Jossey-Bass, 1993 .

O'Hara, N., M. Duvanich, M., Foss, M., N. Wells. "The Vanderbilt Professional Practice Program, Part Two," *Journal of Nursing Administration* (October, 2003): 512.

Phillips, D. T. *Lincoln on Leadership: Executive Strategies for Tough Times.* New York: Time Warner Books, 1992.

Pittam, J., and K.R. Scherer. *Vocal Expression and Communication of Emotion.* In M. Lewis and J.M. Haviland (Eds.) *Handbook of Emotions.* New York: The Guilford Press, 1993.

Porter-O'Grady, T. "Is Shared Governance Still Relevant?" *Journal of Nursing Administration* (October 2001): 468.

Porter-O'Grady, T., and C. Wilson. *The Leadership Revolution in Health Care.* Gaithersburg, MD: Aspen Publishers, 1995.

Post N,. and W. Bellows. "The Principles of Systems Energetics." Training program lecture notes. San Francisco, 1988.

Post, N. "Managing Human Energy: An Ancient Tool of Change Experts." *OD Practitioner* (December 1989).

_____. Course notes. Philadelphia, 1990.

_____. Course notes. Philadelphia, 1993.

_____. "Elements of Organization." Training program lecture notes. Manual published by Post Enterprises, Philadelphia, 1993.

Prochaska, J. *Changing for Good*, New York: Avon Books, 1994.

Reichstein, G. *Wood Becomes Water: Chinese Medicine in Everyday Life.* New York: Kodansha International, Inc., 1998.

Remen, R. *Kitchen Table Wisdom.* New York: Riverhead Books, 1996.

Richardson, C. *Take Time for Your Life.* New York: Broadway Books, 1998.

_____. *Life Makeovers: Improve Your Life One Week at a Time.* New York: Broadway Books, 2000.

Robinson, K., E. Eck, B. Keck, N. Wells. "The Vanderbilt Professional Nursing Practice Program, Part One." *Journal of Nursing Administration* (September 2003): 441.

Steahan, R. "Vanderbilt Professional Nursing Program, Part Three." *Journal of Nursing Administration* (November, 2003): 568–577.

Stolzenberger, K. "Beyond the Magnet Award." *Journal of Nursing Administration* (October, 2003): 522.

Studer, Q. "From Customer Satisfaction to Bottom Line Results." Presentation for American Organization of Nurse Executives annual meeting. Nashville, TN, March 2000.

_____. "Taking Your Organization to the Next Level." Presentation for Tenet Health Care System Southeastern Region Nurse Administrators, June 20, 2002.

Tolle, E. *The Power of Now: A Guide to Spiritual Enlightenment.* Novato CA: New World Library, 1999.

Thompson, D., G. Wolf, and S. J. Spear. "Driving Improvement in Patient Care: Lessons from Toyota." *Journal of Nursing Administration* (November 2003): 585–595.

Whisman, L. "Creating a Culture of Service Excellence." Presentation for Franklin Square Medical Center, June 13, 2002.

Wilson, J.G., and R. Wellins. *Leadership Trapeze: Strategies for Leadership in Team-Based Organizations.* San Francisco: Jossey-Bass Publishers, 1994.

About the Authors

Sharon H. Cox, RN, MSN

Sharon Cox has over thirty-five years experience in health care ranging from staff nurse to unit/program manager to faculty and administrative roles in academic health centers. She was born in Miami, Florida and spent her early years in the Southeast graduating from Georgia Baptist School of Nursing in Atlanta and later received her Masters of Science in Nursing from the Medical College of Georgia in Augusta. Fifteen years in a variety of clinical and management roles provided the basis for becoming an independent consultant with Creative Healthcare in Minneapolis in 1987 and founding Cox & Associates in 1993.

She has conducted workshops and seminars and consulted for nearly 400 hospitals and health care organizations in the United States and Canada. Widely known for her lively and entertaining style of presentation and as an effective facilitator for system-wide culture change, Sharon has published in professional journals and developed training materials in areas of leadership and organizational development, change management and creating a culture for retention. She is a co-author with Shelley Cohen of HCPro's *Nurse Manager Toolkit* and is on the editorial board of *Nursing Management Magazine*.

She has two adult children Christine and Rob and enjoys fly fishing and golf with her husband Jim. They are avid fans of the University of Tennessee football team and live in Nashville, Tennessee with two tom cats, Travis and Casey.

Jo Manion, PhD, RN, CNAA, FAAN

Jo Manion is a speaker, accomplished author and senior management consultant who offers practical and creative approaches to organizational and professional issues. Since the early 1990s she has worked with organizations and individuals engaged in creating effective cultural change, developing leadership capacity and transforming organizational structures. Her focus is on creating positive workplace environments with high impact retention strategies.

As author, her third book, *From Management to Leadership*, was released in 1998 and named by Doody's as one of the best health care titles in both 1998 and 1999. It will be released in its second edition in early summer 2005. She also wrote a book on creating team-based health care organizations and a best-selling and award-winning book about innovation and nurse intrapreneurship. A new book, *Create a Positive Health Care Workplace! Practical Strategies to Retain Today's Workforce and Find Tomorrow's*, will also be released in 2005.

Jo is a fellow in the American Academy of Nursing. She has published dozens of articles and book chapters on current issues in health care. Growing up in the Midwest, her undergraduate and graduate degrees are from Marycrest College and the University of Iowa. Additionally she has a Master's degree and doctorate in Organizational Development from The Fielding Institute. She makes her home in the Orlando area with her husband and their two dogs.

Diane A. Miller, MAOL, RN, BSN

Diane Miller began her consulting career in 1984 by developing creative technologies for improving service and interdepartmental relationships in a large health care system in New Mexico. She developed a positive international reputation in the areas of problem solving, creativity, change management, team design, and leadership effectiveness. Diane is recognized for her practical approach, the depth of her understanding of organization development, and her humorous presentation style.

Diane's work with leadership development in the United Kingdom and Ireland was recognized by Leeds University in Leeds, England with her two-year appointment as a Guest Lecturer. Over 100,000 participants were involved during a two-year period in leadership and facilitator workshops that she developed and coordinated for the National Health Service. She has authored numerous articles for journals in the US, Canada, and England.

Diane received her undergraduate degree at the University of New Mexico and received her Masters of Art in Organizational Leadership from the College of St. Catherine in Minnesota. She spends her leisure hours drawing or writing poetry. She enjoys photography, gardening, and plucking the strings of a guitar.

Ordering Information

Copies of *Natures Wisdom in the Workplace*
may be purchased directly through the publisher.
Email: SynergyPrs@aol.com, or write to: Synergy Press,
10277 Scarborough Road, Bloomington, MN 55437.
Discounts on quantity purchases are available.

Printed in the United States
81228LV00003B/88

9 780976 443506